MW00581698

Your Caption Has Been Selected

Your Caption Has Been Selected

MORE THAN ANYONE COULD POSSIBLY WANT TO
KNOW ABOUT THE NEW YORKER CARTOON
CAPTION CONTEST

Lawrence Wood

FOREWORD BY BOB MANKOFF

ST. MARTIN'S
PRESS
NEW YORK

First published in the United States by St. Martin's Press, an imprint of St. Martin's Publishing Group

www.stmartins.com

Designed by Steven Seighman

The Library of Congress Cataloging-in-Publication Data is available upon request.

ISBN 978-1-250-33340-7 (paper over board)
ISBN 978-1-250-33341-4 (ebook)

Our books may be purchased in bulk for promotional, educational, or business use. Please contact your local bookseller or the Macmillan Corporate and Premium Sales Department at 1-800-221-7945, extension 5442, or by email at MacmillanSpecialMarkets@macmillan.com.

First Edition: 2024

10 9 8 7 6 5 4 3 2 1

My father, a professor at Syracuse University, wrote *Applications of Thermodynamics* and tried to dedicate it to my mother, but she wouldn't let him. "If you write a novel or collection of poems," she said, "you can dedicate it to me, but not a textbook." This isn't a textbook, so I hope my wife won't mind my dedicating it to her and our daughters.

For Gwenan, Miranda, Sasha, and Emily

Contents

Foreword by Bob Mankoff

Some names you instantly associate with *New Yorker* cartoons: Peter Arno, Charles Addams, Roz Chast, Lawrence Wood. Lawrence Wood? Well, maybe not. Or maybe not *yet*.

Lawrence is not a cartoonist. He's a lawyer on the side of the angels, representing people who are living in poverty in Chicago. But he's also the Ken Jennings of *The New Yorker* Cartoon Caption Contest. He's won it the most, he's the best at it, he's the GOAT. And if Lawrence is the Ken Jennings of the contest, I'm the Alex Trebek. The contest was my brainchild. I introduced it in 1999 as a feature of our annual cartoon issue, and I was deeply involved in every aspect of it until I stepped down as cartoon editor in 2017. It's in other capable hands now, but I still think of it as my baby even though it's all grown up.

Its big growth spurt happened in 2005, when the contest went weekly—and viral. Soon, anyone who knew about *The New Yorker* knew about the contest. For subscribers to the magazine it became a must-see feature, the one thing everyone was sure to look at—maybe even before the regular cartoons.

The contest's devotees include the thousands of people who enter every week, the fans who cast more than half a million votes to help select each week's finalists, and everyone who follows the Facebook and Instagram pages and podcast devoted to the contest. The audience for the contest is exponentially larger than the number of entrants. This distinguishes the caption contest from *The New Yorker*'s crossword puzzle and online games, which are popular but only among those who try to solve them. Just as you don't have to be a cartoonist to love and appreciate *New Yorker* cartoons, you don't have to enter the contest to delight in the winners' and finalists' ingenuity and comic chops.

And no one has been better at it—better by a sophisticated, twenty-block, New York City mile—than Lawrence Wood. He's won eight contests, placed second in three more, and placed third in yet another four. He's therefore been a finalist an unprecedented fifteen times. But so what? If you were a fan of *Jeopardy!*, would you read a book about it by Ken Jennings just because he was the undisputed champion? Of course you would. Not only because it might help you win, but because you would want to know how a mind like his works when playing such an entertaining and challenging game. And there would be all the behind-the-scenes, inside-baseball information about him and Alex Trebek.

You don't have to be a *Jeopardy!* fan to see the parallels, but let me spell it out for those of you who still haven't hit the buzzer. While this book is 100 percent written by Lawrence, it was my idea that he should write this book—*must* write this book. I've known and worked with Lawrence for years—as the champion of the caption contest; as the author of an article on how to win the contest for a special cartoon edition of *The New Yorker*; as an "idea man" for *New Yorker* cartoonists; and as the author of more than one hundred caption contest commentaries for my website, CartoonStock.com. With all this, I thought he deserved to be better known for his contributions to, and insights regarding the broader implications of, the caption contest.

When I suggested that he write a book about the contest, he didn't hesitate. In fact, he moved too fast, providing me with a first draft in just ten days. Don't worry. That's not the book you're holding in your hands. While it was a fascinating draft, it was mainly from the perspective of a contestant. The inside-baseball, behind-the-scenes parts—the, if you will, Alex Trebek parts—were missing, as were any reflections on what can be learned from the contest about humor, good writing, creativity, and even what it means to be human in the age of artificial intelligence. They're not missing anymore. I pointed Lawrence toward research studies on linguistics and artificial intelligence that had used data from the contest. I also connected him to *New Yorker* cartoonists whose work had been featured in the contest, to my former assistants who had judged it, and to the computer wizards who crowdsourced it. Back to work he went, and ten days later: voilà! Actually, it took another year, but here it finally is. I hope this book, which Lawrence was born to write, will be an enormous success, and that at some point in the future, under the *Jeopardy!* category "Humorists," the answer will be "He wrote *Your Caption Has Been Selected*."

Introduction

Caption contests are not new. They've been around since the late nineteenth century, and the newspapers and magazines that sponsored them enticed people to enter by offering cash prizes. In 1912, *The San Francisco Call* offered twenty dollars for the best title to a drawing of a woman in a cooking apron sifting tiny, well-dressed men through a pan as if they were flour.

"The title," the editors stated, "must not exceed sixteen words in all—the shorter the better."[1] That's still good advice. Eight years later, the *New-York Tribune* reduced the word limit but increased the prize to $1,000—the equivalent of $15,000 today—which was divided among the winner, who got $500, and two runners-up. "Think of it!" the editor wrote.

> $500.00 in cold cash for writing from one to ten words. Isn't it worth trying? An idea you already have in mind may strike the judges as being the best. . . . Send in as many titles as you want. Send in the first one that occurs to you now. Later you can send in others.[2]

The New Yorker, which has held a weekly caption contest since 2005 (it was initially an annual event), doesn't accept more than one entry per person. Nor does it offer cash prizes. It doesn't have to. The mere prospect of seeing one's name in the magazine—once if you're a finalist, twice if you're a winner—induces thousands of people to enter the contest every week.

Some contestants are famous. Grammy-winning musician Brad Paisley, Oscar-winning composer John Williams, Emmy-winning comedians Zach Galifianakis and Chevy Chase (who once left the magazine's cartoon department "a five-minute phone message . . . with a very long caption suggestion"[3]), and Pulitzer Prize–winning journalist Maureen Dowd have all tried to win. Dowd said, "I felt like Elaine in that *Seinfeld* episode where she kept trying to do a *New Yorker* cartoon, thinking it couldn't be that hard. But it is."[4] Pulitzer Prize–winning film critic Roger Ebert won the contest in 2011, and I'll have more to say about his victory later.

Why do so many people, week after week, enter a contest that offers nothing but bragging rights? Because *The New Yorker* is worth bragging about. Ebert declared his success in the contest "a career milestone" because he could at last say he had appeared in the magazine.[5] For most people there are only two ways into *The New Yorker*: writing a letter that gets published in The Mail,[6] or becoming a finalist in the caption contest. And only the contest gives you the opportunity to claim that *The New Yorker*—which has published every great humor writer from James Thurber and S. J. Perelman and Dorothy Parker to Calvin Trillin and David Sedaris and Tina Fey—found you funny.

The contest is part of the cultural landscape. In 2010, when *New Yorker* editor David Remnick appeared on *The Daily Show* to promote his biography of President

Obama, host Jon Stewart complained that he had never won the magazine's caption contest despite having entered every week for a year. Stewart then showed Remnick three cartoons he had captioned with the same line (*"Well, Obama DID promise us change!"*) and said "There are forty-nine more of those."[7]

New Yorker art critic Peter Schjeldahl incorporated the contest into his review of an Edgar Degas exhibit at the Museum of Fine Arts in Boston. "The show begins with academic figure drawings and two bizarre early history paintings. . . . The first, in which one of a gaggle of semi-nude girls enigmatically thrusts an arm toward a bunch of arrogant nude boys, seems to me a particularly august candidate for the New Yorker cartoon-caption contest: what is she saying?"[8]

In season two of HBO's *Bored to Death*, Ted Danson's character struggles to caption a *New Yorker* cartoon of a police duck talking to a suicidal bear. He briefly considers *"You can bear it"* before giving up and saying, "I'm never going to win this thing." The show's creator, Jonathan Ames, said he wrote that scene because he himself had "failed at the caption contest . . . a number of times." *New Yorker* cartoonist Carolita Johnson subsequently sketched six drawings for the *Bored to Death* cast to caption, but "only Ames was fearless enough to take a stab at them." One cast member declared the challenge "too hard."[9]

How to Write a New Yorker Cartoon Caption, an online video series, featured such celebrities as Danny DeVito, Will Ferrell, Zach Galifianakis, Bill Hader, Ellie Kemper, Nick Kroll, Julia Louis-Dreyfus, Kumail Nanjiani, and Nick Offerman captioning drawings that had appeared in the contest. Another episode featured Alice Kassnove,[10] a nine-year-old girl whose talent for captioning went viral after Emmy-nominated comedy writer Bess Kalb (whose work has appeared in *The New*

Yorker) bragged about her on Twitter: "My cousin's 9-year-old daughter Alice has been quietly and masterfully slaying the @NewYorker's caption contest. . . . There are so many (she grabs every issue before her mom can get ahold of it) and every single one of them is perfect."[11]

When I was Alice's age, in 1971, I hadn't yet discovered *The New Yorker*, but I was obsessed with cartoons and humor. My older sister subscribed to *MAD*, and I studied every issue. When she moved on to *National Lampoon*, which my parents wouldn't let me read, I got my own subscription to *MAD*, which was lowbrow but not shocking. Its most notorious cover was a Norman Mingo painting of a fist with a raised middle finger—nothing compared to *National Lampoon*'s photo of a gun pointed at a dog's head, next to the words, "If You Don't Buy This Magazine, We'll Kill This Dog."

MAD was a terrific showcase for smart and funny comic art, and many *New Yorker* cartoonists loved it as much as I did.

"It made sense to me," said Roz Chast, a staff cartoonist at *The New Yorker* whose work has appeared in the magazine since 1978. "I would watch these shows, these commercials, that were entirely stupid, but I didn't know how to quite voice it. It made me laugh so hard—'Cheese & Sandbag Coffee'! For some reason, that killed me. I liked Don Martin. I liked the fake ads and, of course, Al Jaffee."[12] Jaffee created *MAD*'s Fold-In feature, a back-page drawing with a long caption that could be folded vertically and inward to reveal a hidden picture and shorter caption.

The connection between *MAD* and *The New Yorker* was perhaps best exemplified by Antonio Prohías's wordless comic strip, *Spy vs. Spy*, which *MAD* started publishing in 1961. Prohías died in 1987, but the strip continued without him, and in 1997, future *New Yorker* cartoonist Peter Kuper (with whom I've collaborated on cartoons that have appeared in both *MAD* and *The New Yorker*) started writing and illustrating it.

My love for *MAD*'s "Usual Gang of Idiots," which is what the magazine called its contributing writers and illustrators, eventually led to my obsession with the cartoonists I discovered in my parents' tattered copy of *The New Yorker Twenty-Fifth Anniversary Album*, a hardbound collection of cartoons from 1925 through 1950. That's where I found James Thurber's seal in the bedroom; Charles Addams's family on the roof of their gothic mansion, preparing to dump a cauldron of hot oil on a group of Christmas carolers below; and Peter Arno's patrician snob outside a college football stadium, where he responds to a man who's selling pennants for the two teams (Harvard and Western Maryland) by exclaiming, "*Which* one? *Great heavens, are you* mad?"

My parents subscribed to *The New Yorker*, so I had access to every issue's cartoons, and I quickly became as captivated by Sam Gross, Ed Koren, and Lee Lorenz as I had been by Don Martin, Al Jaffee, and Antonio Prohías. In 1980 I left home for college, where, in the library, I read new issues of *The New Yorker* and discovered more great cartoonists, including Leo Cullum, Mick Stevens, and the man who would eventually suggest I write this book: Bob Mankoff.

By November 22, 1999, when Mankoff introduced the caption contest as an annual event, I had been subscribing to the magazine for years, mostly for the cartoons, and I jumped at the chance to caption this drawing by Jack Ziegler:

I wasn't alone. "By E-mail and by snail mail, by fax and by courier, more than five thousand captions flowed into Contest Headquarters high above midtown Manhattan."[13] We all wanted what the editors described as a "chance to be a cartoonist—or, at least, half of one—and a shot at being published in *The New Yorker*."[14]

It was a dream that wouldn't come true for me for another seven years, long after the magazine had turned the contest into a weekly competition, but I'll never forget the day I finally made it to the finalists' round. Mankoff's assistant called my house while I was at work and told my wife, who was home with our five-year-old daughter Miranda. I then got a call from Mira, who screamed, "Dad! You're a finalist in the caption contest! You're going to be in *The New Yorker*! THE NEW YORKER!" She had never heard of *The New Yorker*, but she liked delivering good news.

Two years later my friend Julie told her neighbor, *Chicago Tribune* reporter Steve Johnson, that I had become a finalist in the contest for the third time. He found that newsworthy and wrote two articles[15] that got me noticed by *Time*,[16] Roger Ebert,[17] and Mankoff. After I secured my fifth victory, Mankoff contacted me.

"I'm sorry," he wrote, "but you've won too many times, so we have to ban you." I told him I understood, and he told me he was kidding. He then asked me to send him ten cartoon concepts a week to see if I could move beyond completing a captionless drawing and actually come up with original ideas. Here are just five of the fifty ideas I sent him:

DRAWING: In an elementary school, a teacher addresses a seven-year-old Jesus.
CAPTION: *"So I don't mix you up with the other one, you'll be Jesus H."*

DRAWING: In the corner of a boxing ring, a trainer is giving advice to a fighter who's taken a beating.
CAPTION: *"When you get back in there, I want you to try reasoning with him."*

DRAWING: While running—along with the rest of his Aztec tribe—from an erupting volcano, a man says something to his friend.
CAPTION: *"I told you she wasn't a virgin."*

DRAWING: Satan addresses a lecture hall full of devils who are holding pitchforks and listening attentively.
CAPTION: *"So to recap, 'Love the sin, hate the sinner.'"*

DRAWING: At an exclusive club, one wealthy member addresses another.
CAPTION: "I *said, 'Life is fair.'*"

Mankoff then connected me to *New Yorker* cartoonists who were interested in collaborating. He also tried to get a sense of how my mind worked by, among other things, asking me to record myself as I came up with entries for each week's caption contest. (He listened to these recordings only after the finalists for each contest had been chosen.) *New Yorker* articles editor Susan Morrison warned me "to be careful, or Mankoff's going to start attaching electrodes to your head."[18]

He never went that far, but after leaving his position as cartoon editor at *The New Yorker* and founding CartoonStock.com, an online archive and store for cartoons,[19] he contacted me with a less radical proposal. He had just started on his website a weekly caption contest that featured drawings by *New Yorker* cartoonists, and he wanted me to review, evaluate, and comment on the entries. After I'd produced more than one hundred of these commentaries, he came up with another proposal: write a book on *The New Yorker* Cartoon Caption Contest. Mankoff soon made it clear, however, that he was envisioning more than a how-to manual for people looking to improve their chances of winning the contest. He wanted a history of the competition as well as an examination of its broader implications for humor, creativity, writing, collaboration, and even artificial intelligence, so that's what this book is about.

That, and how to win the contest.

THE CONTEST

The year 2024 marks the twenty-fifth anniversary of the Cartoon Caption Contest, and over the past quarter-century it's evolved from an interesting experiment to *The New Yorker*'s most popular feature. For the first six years of its existence, it was a once-a-year affair that took the editors more than two months to judge and resulted in not only a winning caption, but as many as seventeen honorable mentions. It was popular but had no wider cultural influence. That quickly changed when the contest became a weekly online competition, with a captionless drawing appearing every Monday morning, the deadline for submissions expiring the following Sunday at midnight, the editors taking a week to choose three finalists, and the public selecting the winner through a popular vote.

The contest soon became both a cultural phenomenon and a source of frustration for Mankoff's assistant, who had only a few days to sift through five thousand to ten thousand entries and find about fifty that were good enough to send to Mankoff for his consideration. To ease the burden, *The New Yorker* started crowdsourcing the contest with the help of a computer system that allows the public to rate entries and moves the most popular ones to the top of a sorted list. Crowdsourcing provides much-needed relief to the cartoon department but also increases the risk of overlooking worthy captions that do not appear among the top two hundred entries. This problem is exacerbated by the fact that not everyone whose votes determine which entries make it to the top of the list is qualified to decide what's best. Nevertheless, crowdsourcing works surprisingly well, and ensures that each week's finalists are generally good and sometimes great.

Before the crowdsourcing process begins, *The New Yorker* must decide which drawing to feature in each contest. I'll explain how that decision gets made and why *The New Yorker* stopped giving each contest-winner a signed print of the cartoon with their caption—a prize that drove a student at one of the nation's top universities to commit a heinous crime.

How It All Began

Mankoff introduced the caption contest as part of *The New Yorker*'s annual Cartoon Issue, and it was judged by the magazine's staff. The initial goal, said Mankoff, "was to create this odd sort of challenge for readers and discover whether the results were interesting. In other words, we wanted to know how inspiration was sparked when someone was looking at an image with an incongruity in it that called out for a comic line."[1]

Many readers came up with funny ideas for each annual contest, including the one featuring this drawing by Mick Stevens:

"People got to some of the main humorous aspects right away," said Mankoff. "Why was the angel in jail? What could an angel have done that was so bad? Would he get time off for good behavior?" But that was just the first step. The real challenge was turning the funny idea into a concise and well-crafted caption. Simon Hatley met that challenge with a practical tip for surviving prison: *"I'd lose the dress."*

The annual contests were popular. This one, featuring a drawing by Danny Shanahan, elicited more than fourteen thousand entries:

New Yorker cartoonist Bob Eckstein remembers entering that contest (long before he started submitting his work to the magazine) but doesn't recall his exact entry. He got a telephone message about his caption from the magazine's cartoon department, but by that time he had learned there was no cash prize so he lost interest in the contest and never returned the call. With Eckstein out of the way, the path was clear for Lauren Helmstetter, of Leawood, Kansas, to take the top spot with, *"You'll feel better when you see the doctor"*—a fine example of transforming an ordinary statement into a joke.

Another annual contest challenged readers to create their own gag cartoon. Charles Barsotti drew the setup—a therapist taking notes next to an empty couch—and supplied eight potential patients (a squirrel, an anthropomorphic screwdriver, a king, a businessman, a woman, a dog, Superman, and a dragon) who could be cut out and placed on the couch. June Anderson and Dr. Alice McKay, of Henderson, Nevada, put the king there and created a sibling rivalry between him and the therapist: *"Mom always liked you best."* Kip Conlon, of Brooklyn, New York, made Superman the patient and filled him with self-doubt: *"Sometimes I think everybody'd be better off if I was a bird or a plane."* But Daniel Adkison, also of Brooklyn, took the prize by having the dog confess, *"I can smell my own fear."*

Relatively few people, only about two thousand, submitted entries to the most challenging annual contest, which completely stumped me. It featured Frank Cotham's drawing of two mechanics relaxing outside their garage while looking at a man who's frantically waving at them from behind the wheel of a car that's speeding round in tight circles. One of the mechanics is calmly commenting on the situation, and Michael Lewis made him philosophical: *"I am reminded that the pleasures of life, like those of travel, lie in the journey rather than the arrival."* David Overman made him slightly more sensitive than his fellow mechanic: *"Come on, just tell him you hear the noise."* But Jennifer Truelove, of Hoboken, New Jersey, won the contest by making him mildly curious: *"At what point does this become our problem?"*

On April 25, 2005, *New Yorker* editor David Remnick turned the contest into a weekly competition. Instead of picking a winning caption, the magazine selected three finalists and let the public choose the victor. The whole process, from printing the drawing to announcing the winning caption, took four weeks—one to submit entries, one to select finalists, one to vote on finalists, and one to count the votes. Here is the winning caption from the first weekly contest, which featured a cartoon by Mike Twohy:[2]

"More important, however, is what I learned about myself."

Roy Futterman, New York City

When Twohy's cartoon appeared in *The New Yorker* as a captionless drawing, it took up the whole back page of the magazine. By the time it reappeared with Futterman's winning caption,[2] it shared space with two other cartoons at different stages of the judging process. One was a Jack Ziegler cartoon that had been featured as a captionless drawing two weeks earlier and now appeared above the three entries that had been selected as finalists. The other was a captionless cartoon by David Sipress. From that point on, every issue afforded readers an opportunity to enjoy or resent the winning caption in one contest, vote for their favorite finalist, and submit an entry for the current competition.

Choosing the Drawings

Like most drawings that appear in the contest, this one by Mankoff originally had a caption:

"Sorry, hard-ons, the ballbusters have it."

That line didn't make it past the censors, so Mankoff removed it and used the image for the contest. The winning entry then turned his drawing into one of the best single-panel cartoons I've seen:

"Well, then, it's unanimous."
Anne Whiteside, San Francisco, Calif.

Sometimes a cartoonist will submit a captionless drawing to *The New Yorker* for inclusion in the contest. Robert Leighton did it only once:

"The drawing almost worked by itself," he said, "but it would be funnier with a caption and since I knew there was nothing more I could add, I let it become someone else's problem." The winning entry, from Ken Park, of San Francisco, California, was a reference to daily crossword puzzles that get increasingly difficult as the week progresses: "*Why couldn't he have been murdered on a Monday?*"

Leighton thinks the editors have, "for the most part, chosen wisely when they've decided to remove the caption from one of my cartoons and use the drawing for the contest." But not always. Years ago he submitted this cartoon to *The New Yorker*:

"My next-door neighbor! And my next-door neighbor's wife!"

It didn't sell, so three years later he resubmitted the same drawing with a different caption: *"My God! How long has this been going on?"* The magazine removed the caption and used the image for the contest. The editors then selected the following three submissions as finalists, and the first two were nearly identical to Leighton's original captions:

"How long has this been going on?"
Jeff Green, Brooklyn, N.Y.

"Oh, no! My best friend and my best friend's wife!"
Mark Campos, Seattle, Wash.

"Interested in a threesome? I'll just sit on the floor and sort tax receipts."
Kathy Kinsner, New York City

To Leighton's surprise, the third entry won the popular vote.

In a 2005 interview with Ben Greenman, an editor at *The New Yorker*, Mankoff explained that some drawings work better than others for the contest.[1]

Greenman: Let's talk a bit about the images you're picking. There are certain kinds of cartoons that wouldn't work at all for this contest. There's a famous *New Yorker* cartoon that you actually drew. The caption is "*No, Thursday's out. How about never—is never good for you?*" But the image is just a man on a phone at a desk. It seems like that wouldn't work.

Mankoff: It wouldn't. People would just send in their generically funny man-on-phone lines, and we'd have no real standard for judging one against the other. Many would be funny in their own way, but there would be no competition between entries, no common ground, and, as a result, no contest. Now, if instead of the receiver he had a banana in his hand—

Greenman: Yes?

Mankoff: Well, maybe that wouldn't be so good. But a banana at least puts us on the right road. You need some sort of incongruous element.

There was no incongruous element in Drew Dernavich's drawing of two men stuck in a traffic jam, so it was particularly hard to caption:

Dernavich's original caption was interesting—"*What if traffic isn't* them, *Martin. What if traffic is* us?"—but I won the contest with something less philosophical: "*Try honking again.*"

Choosing the Finalists

It was initially the responsibility of Mankoff's assistant to handle the first phase of judging each week's contest by spending hours reviewing all five thousand to ten thousand entries and culling them down to the top fifty or so. Mankoff then picked the ten best, sent them to the magazine's editors (who rated them "funny," "somewhat funny," or "not funny"), tabulated their responses, and selected three finalists from those that came out on top. The finalists used to get a call, but now they receive a congratulatory email that begins with the title of this book: "Your caption has been selected." The contest is judged blindly, so the finalists' identities are revealed only after their captions are chosen.

The assistants who reviewed or are still reviewing the contest entries deserve recognition: Andy Friedman, Marshall Hopkins, Zachary Kanin, Farley Katz, Adam Moerder, Jennifer Saura, Marc Philippe Eskenazi, Colin Stokes, and Rachel Perlman.

Andy Friedman is an artist and musician who worked for Mankoff when the caption contest was still an annual event, and his cartoons have appeared in *The New Yorker* since 1999. Initially they were published under the pseudonym "Larry

Hat" because Friedman worried that people might take his art less seriously if they knew he was funny. His later work appeared under his own name:

"Recommend? No. But there are plenty of dishes this evening that I'd dare you to eat."

Marshall Hopkins and Jen Saura have also had their cartoons published in *The New Yorker*:

Midas Loses His Touch

"I stopped by the orphanage on my way home."

SAURA

Zachary Kanin, a former staff writer for *Saturday Night Live* and the co-creator of *I Think You Should Leave with Tim Robinson*,[1] is a cartoonist whose drawings appear both in the magazine,

"A heart would be great, sure, but what I'd really like is a working human penis."

and in the caption contest:

"She left me for an engine that could."

Alexander Toth, Boston, Mass.

To survive the process of reviewing thousands of contest entries week after week, Kanin uploaded them into a spreadsheet, ordered them by length, eliminated all the jokes about the insurance company Geico ("There were always about five hundred submissions that were like, "Good news. Now you're getting a better deal through Geico."[2]), and ordered the remaining entries by common phrases so it was easier to spot the best version of the same joke. Still, he said, "I thought I was going to die."[3]

Like Kanin, Farley Katz is a cartoonist whose work appears both in the magazine,

"Just in case the conference call runs long."

and in the contest:

"Matisse now; Pollock later."
Mark Laurent Asselin, Bethesda, Md.

I asked him how he feels when *The New Yorker* removes his caption from a cartoon and uses the drawing for the contest. "Hurt," he said. "Then honored. Finally, aroused. Sorry, what was the question? Honestly, I'm always excited to see what great jokes people will come up with. I love seeing caption writers take my drawings to entirely new and unexpected places." As for trying to caption a drawing in the contest that's by another cartoonist, "I never click submit, but after years of reading thousands of entries I dream in captions and can't help but write down a few ideas when I see the latest contest."

Katz and the writer Simon Rich, who often contributes to *The New Yorker*, collaborated on *The Married Kama Sutra: The World's Least Erotic Sex Manual*, and claim they collaborated on cartoons the magazine's editors rejected. During an appearance on *Running Late with Scott Rodowsky*, they presented a few of their alleged submissions, including a cartoon that's set in a restroom where two janitors are holding mops and high-fiving each other as they stand by a toilet. One janitor says, "*Yeah—we are gonna clean* the shit *out of this thing.*" According to Katz and Rich, that cartoon failed to appear in *The New Yorker* only because the editors did not understand how it worked on multiple levels. Other cartoons of theirs, they said, were so filthy they could reveal nothing but the captions: "*That's not yogurt,*" "*That's not ice cream,*" and "*I've said it before and I will say it again— that's a lot of feces.*"

Adam Moerder contributed short pieces to the magazine, including reports from the annual New Yorker Festival. My favorite highlighted the difference between heroes and anti-heroes by providing several examples, including this one:

An oblong roll filled with various meats, cheeses, vegetables, spices, and sauces: Hero
Bread stuffed inside a slab of ham: Anti-hero[4]

Marc Philippe Eskenazi is a writer whose short humor pieces, including "Thank You for the Forty-Eight Cruise-Ship Brochures," have appeared in *The New Yorker*. He's also a musician, so Mankoff had him judge the magazine's Caption Contest Song Contest.[5] The winning entry came from Seth Wittner, of Henderson, Nevada, who set his song to the tune of Creedence Clearwater Revival's "Proud Mary." Here's a sample lyric:

> *If you make us laugh, and you ain't on our staff*
> *Then you are in the runnin' for a finalist's place.*

Eskenazi performed a rendition of Wittner's song in a music video directed by Myles Kane,[6] who went on to make "Voyeur," the acclaimed documentary about motel owner Gerald Foos, who built an "observation deck" above his motel rooms so he could spy through ceiling vents on the guests below.

Eskenazi has also come up with ideas for *New Yorker* cartoonists Benjamin Schwartz and Liam Francis Walsh:

"Get A Tomb!"

Though he does draw, Eskenazi prefers to collaborate because he's a better writer than artist. Here's one of his cartoons:

His caption—"*When*"—appears very faintly at the top. Benjamin Schwartz liked the concept so he redrew the cartoon, turning the creature into an overcaffeinated man, and submitted it to *The New Yorker*. The magazine bought the drawing for the contest and subsequently chose the caption it had removed as one of the three finalists:

"Quick, before Bloomberg bans it!"
Rita Costanzo, Staten Island, N.Y.

"When."
Victoria Rice, New York City

"Best decaf in town, Dolores."
Krista Van Wart, Brooklyn, N.Y.

Rita Costanzo's joke about Bloomberg won the popular vote, and the mayor, who once complained that no matter how hard he tried he could never make the finalists' round in the caption contest,[7] bought a print and hung it in his office.

Colin Stokes worked for both Mankoff and the current cartoon editor, Emma Allen, and he appeared with one or the other of them in five seasons of *The New Yorker* video series, *The Cartoon Lounge*. He is also a writer whose humor pieces, including "Things Other Than a Bouquet to Toss Over Your Shoulder at a Wedding and What They Mean for Whoever Catches Them," have been published in *The New Yorker*.

Rachel Perlman was initially Colin's assistant, but when he left the magazine she assumed his role as the associate cartoon editor. Before joining the staff, she won the caption contest featuring this Charlie Hankin cartoon:

"*They did say ocean views.*"

Rachel Perlman, New York City

It was the only time she entered the contest.

Crowdsourcing

In *Very Semi-Serious*, an HBO documentary on *New Yorker* cartoons, Zachary Kanin said that reviewing thousands of captions each week was "fun, but also soul crushing." The excruciating nature of the task was exacerbated by the fact that many of the entries were mediocre or worse. In 2016, therefore, *The New Yorker* turned to crowdsourcing, which involves a machine learning system called NEXT that uses algorithms to sort through massive amounts of crowdsourced data. Developed by Robert Nowak, an engineering professor at the University of Wisconsin, it has many applications, and Mankoff used it to make his assistants' jobs easier. "We crowd-source the judging of the initial phase of the contest," he wrote, "because it would be impossible for one person or even a number of persons to look at more than five thousand entries and not become completely numb to humor."[1]

NEXT enables anyone interested in the contest to rate entries—as few or as many as they choose. It then collects those ratings and ranks the submissions according to an algorithm that over time pushes more successful captions to the top of a sorted list. The first crowdsourced contest appeared on March 21, 2016. In a *Cartoon Lounge* video, Mankoff explained that he and Colin Stokes and the magazine's editors would still be involved in choosing the three finalists. Crowdsourcing, however, would give the public a chance to participate in the first stage of the selection process.[2]

If you start voting on Monday—right after the submission deadline—you'll see many terrible jokes, but as the week progresses and the algorithm starts separating the wheat from the chaff, you start to see fewer dreadful entries (bad puns, captions with unnecessary exclamation points) and more good-to-great submissions. Once the captions are ranked, the cartoon department selects the ten best, sends them to the editorial staff at *The New Yorker*, tabulates their responses, and chooses the three finalists.

Some *New Yorker* cartoonists look at the crowdsourced entries for contests that feature their drawings. Ellis Rosen likes to "see if there is a common theme among the ideas and how many of them are similar to my original caption. It's also fun to see angles I never even considered."

A caption has a significantly better chance of attracting *The New Yorker*'s attention if it appears among the top two hundred entries. A random sample of twenty consecutive contests (Nos. 811 to 830) revealed that all but one of the sixty finalists were in the top two hundred. The outlier was the winning caption from a contest that featured this cartoon by Paul Karasik:

"*It leaves me feeling empty.*"
Jesse Spain, Palo Alto, Calif.

That caption came in 416th out of more than 6,400 entries, which is impressive (top 7 percent), but *The New Yorker* rarely digs that deep for a finalist. It usually doesn't have to. Crowdsourcing ensures that many of the best captions rise, if not to the top, then pretty close to it.

The process therefore has two advantages: it results in generally strong finalists, and it relieves any one person of the weekly and mind-numbing task of reading thousands of alarmingly bad captions in search of the relatively few gems. But there are drawbacks.

Crowdsourcing encourages voters to rate entries quickly, and therefore favors captions that are short and simple (puns, for example) over more interesting jokes that require a little thought. It also increases the risk of overlooking a truly fine caption—the kind that, instead of making you think "yeah, that works," actually makes you laugh—because it didn't appear high enough on the crowdsourced list. Finally, the process is too democratic. Anyone can be a judge, and not everyone is qualified. That's why the top-rated entries include, along with many of the best submissions, a good number of the worst.

Contest No. 827, for instance, featured this cartoon by Lars Kenseth:

It elicited nearly six thousand entries, and the top one hundred included many that were great and some that were not:

GREAT	NOT SO GREAT
I'm an anesthesiologist.	*Where do you kill your clothes?*
You won't believe how long I've been waiting for this train.	*Wait—'B.C.' means business casual?*
I gave you the wheel and this is what you did with it?	*Dress for the job you want.*
No one says anything when I jump over the turnstile.	*You know, I invented the man cave.*
This is the club car.	*I'm out clubbing.*
How do you kill your lunch with that thing?	*I prefer the term 'cave person.'*
Actually, I'm from the future.	*I'm from the future. Vote carefully.*
So you take everything they've got but don't get to hit them?	*I'm still paying off my student loans.*
You must be a gatherer.	*It's okay, I have an open carry permit.*
I still say rock beats paper.	*True, paper covers rock, but rock beats lawyer.*

Is There a Prize?

When Roger Ebert won the caption contest in 2011, he wrote, "I don't know what the prize is. Glory, I suppose."[1] Actually, the prize was a signed print of the cartoon with the winning caption. In 2016, however, *The New Yorker* got rid of that prize so more people could enter the contest.

"For reasons too complicated to go into here," Mankoff wrote, "the awarding of a prize . . . creates legal issues that make it difficult to have citizens from certain countries enter. Also, the prize prevents anyone under eighteen from entering."[2] Mankoff later tried, without success, to provide a more detailed explanation in a *Cartoon Lounge* video:[3] "There are so many arcane rules in different countries about prizes. . . . In Europe, a problem is with data storage and I don't even know what that problem is." Turning to his assistant, Colin Stokes, he asked, "Do you have any idea?"

Colin, who's from England, said, "I think it's because the data has an odd accent."

"Oh, you should talk," said Mankoff.

Before *The New Yorker* eliminated the prize, I won signed cartoons by Tom Cheney, Leo Cullum, Drew Dernavich, John Klossner, Danny Shanahan, Mick Stevens, and Jack Ziegler. They're worth a lot to me and apparently to others. Someone stole my Ziegler print during the University of Chicago's annual, four-day scavenger hunt called Scav, which challenges teams to earn points by finding or building unusual items.[4] Item No. 137 on the 2012 Scavenger Hunt List was "a signed cartoon print received for winning the *New Yorker* cartoon caption competition." It was worth fifteen points, more than most of the other 350 items on the list.

Three teams contacted me and asked if they could borrow my prints for the competition. After Scav ended, the team that borrowed the Ziegler print told me someone had stolen it. I thought I'd never see it again, but two years later I received at my office a FedEx package containing the stolen print with a handwritten note from someone claiming they saw the framed cartoon in a thrift store in Seattle, Washington, and wanted to return it to its rightful owner. Using the tracking number, I checked the FedEx website and discovered that the package came not from Seattle but from Hyde Park, where the University of Chicago is located. The thief, whom I assume was a U of C student, lied about the thrift store and probably just got tired of explaining why they owned a cartoon Ziegler had inscribed to me.

Variations on a Theme

By 2013, the weekly caption contest was such a success that Mankoff held another cartoon-related competition and challenged readers to come up with a cartoon idea based on a cliché. A *New Yorker* cartoonist would then draw up the winning concept.[1]

After the competition ended in a three-way tie,[2] Mankoff reported that "while many people shared my opinion that the finalists were funny, some women took umbrage at this cartoon:"[3]

" SO, SHORT STORY LONG . "

That drawing, by Liam Francis Walsh, was based on my concept, and, as Mankoff noted, not everyone cared for it:

CAROLYNSTACK:

The "short story long" is offensive. Think, would it have worked if the genders were reversed? No!

SISTERACT:

I agree with carolynstack. This type of humor is a hangover from the 1950s and about as stale as it gets. Men actually talk more than women, by the way, according to quantification studies.

With the help of a Leo Cullum cartoon, Mankoff defended my joke:

Long story short, most comedy is based on the predictability of types. And the types, whether they are dumb bosses, greedy bankers, callous doctors, scheming lawyers, or talkative women and insensitive preoccupied husbands, are never good types. Humor doesn't praise. To get a joke, you do not have to believe that the typecasting is accurate. Rather, you just have to be aware of it. And, if there isn't at least a grain of truth behind the typecasting, the joke won't work. Case in point:

Despite the controversy, Mankoff declared the cliché contest a "rousing success" and held yet another cartoon-related competition, this time challenging readers to come up with an image for the caption, *We will always have Paris.*[4] The following week he reviewed several entries for this reverse caption contest.[5]

The "good then, bad now" sentiment in "we'll always have Paris" was characteristic of many contest entries, including this one:

A baguette and cheese are walking down the street in New York City. Restaurant signs advertise "Gluten-Free Bakery" and "Vegan Cafe." Baguette says to Cheese, *"We'll always have Paris."*

An edgier version of this idea was the submission that had Adolf Hitler saying the caption to the Vichy Prime Minister Pétain, as Allied airplanes are seen in the distance.

Several people sent in Paris Hilton jokes, and Mankoff highlighted mine:

A reporter from TMZ is sitting at his desk and addressing the cameras. Behind him on a large TV screen is an image of Paris Hilton and some headline describing her latest scandalous behavior. The reporter is saying, *"We will always have Paris."*

Mankoff did not, however, think my entry was the best overall. The best idea, he wrote, came from Jean Pyle, of Hawthorne, New Jersey, who suggested using the "Paris" caption for an Emily Flake cartoon that had appeared in Contest No. 303:

"We'll always have Paris."

The original winning caption for Flake's drawing was by James Clements, of Culpeper, Virginia: *"Who has the time anymore? Now it just sits there, gathering dust."*

My favorite "always have Paris" cartoon came not from the reverse caption contest but from Sam Gross, and it appeared in *The New Yorker* on February 11, 2008:

"We will always have Paris."

Gross, who died on May 6, 2023, hated the caption contest. "You will never see one of my cartoons in the contest," he said. "I don't want some dentist in Toledo captioning my work."[6] His antipathy toward the competition was noted even in his *New York Times* obituary:

Mr. Mankoff said that Mr. Gross flatly refused to participate in *The New Yorker*'s caption contest. . . . "He basically said, 'If you're not going to let somebody write the last paragraph to an Updike article, you're not doing anything to my caption.'"[7]

It may seem odd to include in my celebration of the contest a cartoon from its most outspoken critic, but I love the contest and Sam Gross equally.

HOW TO WIN THE CONTEST

The New Yorker's current cartoon editor, Emma Allen, regularly meets people who, after confessing that they read the magazine only for the cartoons, launch into "a harangue about the injustice of never having won the caption contest."[1] Mankoff, who started all the trouble by creating the competition, is no stranger to such complaints. In an episode of *The Cartoon Lounge*, he reported that most of the mail he received came from people who were upset they didn't win.[2] He then read from a letter he got from a particularly sore loser:

> *I've been sending in entries for probably four and a half months, none of which have been selected. And almost every single group of finalists is totally juvenile, the complete antithesis of what I would normally expect from your publication. Do you just continuously turn to your interns or your assistants for picking these things? I mean really, I thought* The New Yorker *had a little bit higher standard of intellect. But perhaps, in this day and time, the caption contest is just a game to be toyed with.*

"The contest *is* a game," Mankoff conceded, but it is "very, very hard."

Here's how hard it is: five to ten thousand people enter every week. If you enter the contest just by chance, your odds are one in five thousand. If you did that for one thousand contests, your odds of winning would be 20 percent, and you would have died a long time ago. So, that is not the course you should take. You should try to be funny. Who's really good at this? Lawrence Wood.

Mankoff thinks people can learn from what I've done, so I'll devote the rest of this very long section to specific advice on how to win the contest. Take my advice with a grain of salt. Though I hold the captioning record, I've been a finalist in fewer than 2 percent of the contests. If you want to improve your chances of winning without reading my advice, do what Mankoff suggests: be funnier and enter more often.[3]

Who's Talking?

Harold Ross, *The New Yorker*'s co-founder and editor in chief, held weekly art meetings at which he inspected and evaluated hundreds of cartoon submissions. Pointing at one with his white knitting needle,[1] he would sometimes ask, "Who's talking?"[2]

It's the fundamental question—one that Timothy Tanner, who made it to the finalists' round in 2005, always asks himself when trying to come up with a good caption. "As a threshold matter," he said, "I try to figure out who the hell is supposed to be talking. It's not always immediately apparent."[3] He's right. Here are just three of the more than 6,200 entries that were submitted for the contest that featured this cartoon by Suerynn Lee:

"My ex-wife got most of the house."
"I'm not seeing anyone right now."
"Mexico paid for it."

Those captions were all among the top fifty entries in crowdsourcing, and they would deserve such high rankings if the man with the brick wall on his shoulders were talking, but he isn't. When a cartoon has two characters and only one of them has a mouth, assume the one with the mouth is delivering the line that will serve as your caption. Amy Harr, of Riverside, Connecticut, made the correct assumption when she submitted the winning entry: *Do you mind if I bounce something off you?*

Sometimes both characters have mouths, but it's hard to tell which one is open:

The catcher's mouth is obscured by his mask, and the caveman's mouth is hidden behind a full beard. If you look closely, though, you can see the top half of the catcher's open mouth behind the steel wire frame of his mask, which confirms that he's speaking. John Fistere, of El Cajon, California, looked closely and won the contest with, *"A lot has happened since your last at-bat."*

On one occasion, even *The New Yorker* couldn't decide who was talking. Here are the three captions the editors selected as finalists for the contest featuring this drawing by Zachary Kanin:

"Oh, yeah, we go way back."
Patricia Radosevich-Coia, Reno, Nev.

"He says he is known by many names."
George Nikas, Avondale Estates, Ga.

"Sir, the competition is here to discuss the merger."
Tom Alburn, Wrightsville, Pa.

The first caption had the devil speaking, while the next two had the secretary talking. The voters identified the speaker correctly (it's the secretary) by choosing Tom Alburn's entry as the winning caption.

This drawing by Kaamran Hafeez

presented a special challenge because the woman's mouth appeared to be closed and the knight's was hidden behind his helmet. Based on their postures, and because the knight was holding a document and looking up at the woman, I assumed the knight was speaking and submitted, *"Let me tell you about hostile work environments."* The magazine's editors went in the other direction, selecting three finalists that had the woman addressing the knight, but Hafeez says they got it wrong. "The knight is speaking to the woman," he told me. "The original caption, by my frequent collaborator, Al Batt, was, *'I am* not *getting another paper cut.'*"

There was nothing confusing about this drawing by Ellis Rosen:

The deliveryman was clearly speaking, but some of the top-rated entries got that aspect of the drawing wrong:

"Funny how we never get the same delivery guy."
"John will pay you. That's John on the end."
"And could you get us some napkins?"
"You want a tip? Don't look down."
"Could you also take our picture?"

Despite doing well in crowdsourcing—all five captions were among the top one hundred entries in a contest that elicited more than 5,700 submissions—they could not be selected as finalists because they misidentified the speaker. The winning entry, from Ryan Kendall, of Novato, California, identified him correctly: *"We usually don't deliver above Eighty-second Street."*

What's Happening?

In 2004, when the contest was still an annual event, it featured this drawing by Alex Gregory:

Mistaking the mantle and stabilizing fin for a chef's hat, the editorial staff assumed that the giant squid worked at the sushi bar. So did many of the more than thirteen thousand entrants, including contest-winner Dan Heath and the two runners-up:

"He feels he can do more good working within the system."
Dan Heath, Boston, Mass.

"Actually, he loves the job—it's the commute that drives him crazy."
Sarah Knight, Atlanta, Ga.

"Elusive? He's here every night."
Dennis Christie, New York City

Gregory says they all got it wrong. "Not a hat. Not an employee. Simply a terrifying menu item." To prove his point, Gregory sent me a terrifying photo of a giant squid attacking a whale. The winning caption, Gregory said, should have been, *"Tonight's specials are yellowtail, toro, and S-Q-U-I-D."*

Now take a look at the winning caption from the contest that featured this Sam Hurt cartoon and elicited more than ten thousand entries:

"He says making lemonade is not an option."
Suzan Stodder, Madison, Wis.

It works because the Grim Reaper is handing the man a plate of lemons, but I mistook the bitter fruit for scones and came up with five captions that made no sense:

"He spent all day in the kitchen. The least I can do is vote against the gun bill."
"The Coalition to Stop Gun Violence never brought us warm scones."
"Anyone can make a mistake, and look what he brought us."
"Delicious, with just a hint of bitter almonds."
"Fine. More for me."

Only after I submitted *"Fine. . . ."* did my friend Chris point out my error and say he was submitting, *"Let's give these to Larry Wood and tell him they're scones."*

About a year later, Chris's wife, Alice, told me I had misinterpreted this cartoon by Mick Stevens, which appeared in Contest No. 838:

I assumed the beasts were dinosaurs, and that the one holding a flashlight was telling a scary story. Because dinosaurs had nothing to fear but the huge asteroid that wiped them out, I submitted, *"It was ten miles wide and hurtling through space. . . ."* Alice said my entry made no sense because the beasts were not dinosaurs but dragons, as evidenced by their pointy tails.

At the time, I was interviewing Mick Stevens for this book, so I asked him to settle the issue. It felt like that scene in *Annie Hall*, where Woody Allen gets Marshall McLuhan to resolve Allen's debate with a pompous Columbia University professor who's expounding on McLuhan's work. McLuhan sides with Allen, who turns to the camera and says, "Boy, if life were only like this." For a brief moment it was, but then Stevens told me Alice was right. He also shared his original caption—*"Nope. You're no scarier than you ever were."*—proving that I not only misinterpreted the cartoon but misidentified the speaker.

Looks Matter

The person (or butterfly or whale or boa constrictor) who's speaking may look depressed or angry or elated, and your caption should match that expression. It should also be consistent with every other character's expression. Consider this drawing by Bob Eckstein, which appeared in Contest No. 825:

The pumpkin at the head of the table is talking and smiling, but every other pumpkin looks worried. The best entries addressed this discrepancy:

"I'd like to bring in a consultant. His name is Peter Peter . . . something or other."
"Let's turn those frowns into smiles. Who has a knife?"
"At the end of this month, you're all getting canned."
"Come on, we've all faced cuts before."

Unfortunately, none of those four captions was selected as a finalist. Each was, however, among the top one hundred entries in a contest that elicited more than eight thousand submissions—evidence that crowdsourcing works fairly well.

Everything Matters

Everything that appears in a drawing is important. The cartoonist put it there for a reason and you shouldn't ignore it, but many contestants disregard this rule. Here was my competition in the finalists' round for the contest that featured this cartoon by Carolita Johnson:

"What happened to the mouse that came in before me?"
Tyler Bradley, Stratford, Ont.

"You don't understand. I need people to like me."
Lawrence Wood, Chicago, Ill.

"This is the only place I'm allowed on the couch."
Beth Lawler, Montclair, N.J.

The mouse joke didn't address the dog, and the couch joke didn't address the cat, but my caption addressed both. Still, I expected the couch joke to win because it's funny and came from Beth Lawler, who's well known in the captioning community. She runs a Facebook page—"New Yorker Cartoon Caption Contest Rejects (and Enthusiasts)"—that has more than eight thousand members, and she co-hosts, with contest-winners Vin Coca and Paul Nesja, the *New Yorker Cartoon Caption Contest Podcast.*

This was the third time Beth had been a finalist, and if she won it would be her second victory. I thought she *would* win because her caption was funny and the thousands of people on her Facebook page can vote. She came in second, though, and I suspect her mistake was ignoring the cat. Her joke would have worked just as well (maybe even better) if the therapist were a person, but it was a cat and that aspect of the cartoon had to be addressed.

Details, Details

Though I just wrote that everything in a drawing matters, you can ignore minor details without reducing your chances of getting selected as a finalist. Sometimes, however, highlighting a seemingly insignificant detail can distinguish your entry from the thousands you're competing against and catch the editors' attention. It's an unexpected and, on occasion, surprisingly effective strategy.

It worked for Peter Orum, of Sydney, Australia, who made it to the finalists' round in the contest featuring this drawing by Farley Katz:

His entry—*"You missed your forehead."*—focused on two small worry lines on the man's brow, a detail that escaped almost everyone else's attention. (Just eighteen of the more than 5,800 entries went after the same joke.) My caption—*"I'll fold."*—was also selected as a finalist, but both Orum and I lost the popular vote to Kara Nagle, of Portland, Oregon, who suggested the woman could look beyond appearances: *"Don't worry, I'll still love you when you have wrinkles."*

Tell a Story

This drawing by Gahan Wilson demanded a caption that addressed both boxing and giants:

Because the referee is gesturing toward one of the fighters, my first thought was, *"And, in this corner, weighing in at 5,500 pounds . . ."* Then I wondered what the referee might be saying to the boxers. He's at risk of being stepped on and squashed to death, so I had him say, *"And no fancy footwork."* Next, I focused on the referee's upraised arm, which makes him look like he's reaching for the microphone that descends from the ceiling to the ring. What if one of the boxers had grabbed this microphone by its cord and was dangling it high above the referee as a joke? The referee might then say, *"Very funny. Now give me the microphone."*

I worried that my first idea (*"And, in this corner"*) was too obvious. *The New Yorker* was likely to receive hundreds of similar entries. There are few things more frustrating, at least in the context of the contest, than submitting a caption that is similar or even identical to the winning entry. I considered my remaining two options and went with the line about the microphone because I thought it was unusual and would stand out. I became a finalist but lost the popular vote to Tim Herbert, of Plainfield, New Hampshire, who submitted, *"And in this corner, also hailing from Chernobyl . . ."* My friend Ben consoled me by saying, "You should have submitted the footwork caption. It was funnier."

Losing hurt because I have loved Wilson's cartoons since the mid-'70s. I found them in my parents' *New Yorker*s, my sister's *National Lampoon*s, and the *Playboy* magazines I stole from the mailboxes of the customers on my paper route—a federal crime I justified on the grounds that my victims were married men who could see a naked woman whenever they wanted to.

Herbert's winning entry was similar to one I chose not to submit (*"And, in this corner, weighing in at 5,500 pounds . . ."*) but far better. My caption addressed the boxers' size, but Herbert explained how they got so big. In other words, he told a story.

So did Clinton Guthrie, who won the contest featuring this drawing by Mick Stevens:

"*Getting past the guard is easy. How do we remove the paintings?*"
Clinton Guthrie, New York City

With just twelve words Guthrie turned the cave into a museum, the seated cave-man into a security guard, the cave paintings into valuable works of art, and the spying couple into a pair of thieves planning their next job. I supervised Clint when he worked as an attorney in Chicago, so I like to think I taught him everything he knows about both the law and captioning.

Put Yourself in the Story

According to legend, William Tell was arrested for openly defying Habsburg rule and ordered to use his crossbow to shoot an apple off the head of his young son. Contest No. 725 featured Lars Kenseth's take on this legend and replaced the apple with a tiny cherry:

Looking at this drawing as an outside observer, it's hard to think of a good caption. (It's easy to imagine the boy saying, "Don't do it!" or "Jesus, dad, I'm your son!," but those lines won't get your name in *The New Yorker*.) Pretend you're the boy. Why are you there? What are you thinking? What are you saying? Imagining yourself reacting to a given situation, instead of simply describing what's happening, will help you think of captions.

If you were the boy, you might try to dissuade your father from taking the shot by playing on his insecurities as a parent:

1. *"This is why mom only lets you see me on the weekends."*
2. *"I now see why you only get me every other weekend."*

If that didn't work, you might suggest a bigger target:

1. *"I want to change my answer. My favorite food is watermelon."*
2. *"I say we wait until apples are back in season."*
3. *"You know, pumpkins are in season, too."*

Or otherwise improve your chances of survival:

1. *"Like you always say, Dad, 'Aim high.'"*
2. *"Dad! Glasses!"*

Or suggest a different activity:

1. *"Let's try the Diet Coke and Mentos challenge instead."*
2. *"You know, other dads just play catch."*

Or apologize for an earlier slight: *"I changed my mind, Dad. The skirt looks good on you."*

I can't take credit for those captions—all were among the top one hundred entries in crowdsourcing—but they demonstrate the benefit of putting yourself in the shoes of the character who's speaking. I suspect that's what Emily Shallcross, of Northampton, Massachusetts, did before winning the contest by explaining exactly why the boy was questioning his father's judgment: *"I'm just saying, after this haircut, it's difficult to trust you."*

Spin Straw into Gold

T ry submitting an ordinary statement that takes on an entirely new meaning within the context of the cartoon:

"All his pitches have been inside."
Ben Fishel, Washington, D.C.

"I found something serious under the hood."
Russell Keen, Paris, France

I used that same strategy in Contest No. 786, which featured this drawing by Pia Guerra and Ian Boothby:

Though I made it to the finalists' round with, *"He'll negotiate, but he won't beg,"* I lost the popular vote to Kenny Moore, of Rocklin, California, who transformed an ordinary statement into an even better caption: *"My client is prepared to walk."*

Make a List

Paul Nesja co-hosts the caption contest podcast and has been a finalist nine times. When he's struggling to caption a cartoon, Paul creates a text document and makes a column for every disparate frame of reference. In each column he types out as many relevant words and concepts as he can. He then comes up with captions that reconcile the disparate elements. Here's what such a document might have looked like for the contest featuring P. C. Vey's drawing of a space alien reading a bedtime story to an alarmed girl:

ALIENS	BEDTIME STORIES	BABYSITTERS
Invasion	Goodnight Moon	Parents
Flying saucer	Goodnight air	Time for bed
UFO	H. G. Wells	You need your sleep
Abduction	Technical manual	Monster under the bed
E.T.	Scary	Monster in the closet
Black holes	Stephen King	Stay in bed
Probe	Whitley Strieber	Sweet dreams
Little green men	Goldilocks	Nightmares
Close encounters	Very Hungry Caterpillar	Parents went out
Light-years	Boy Who Cried Wolf	Parents coming home
War of the Worlds	Oh, the Places You'll Go	Parents not coming home

Creating a list can help you identify and then connect every important aspect of the cartoon and come up with a caption that works. But turning such a caption into one *The New Yorker* might select as a finalist (or that gives you good cause to curse the magazine for overlooking your entry) requires you to go a step further and actually be funny.

Make 'Em Laugh

The caption contest is a puzzle, and I'm impressed by anyone who solves it with a well-written sentence or two, but the best winning entries are also funny. When someone reads your caption, you don't want them to stroke their chin and think, "Well done." You want them to laugh.

Not everyone agrees with me on this point. After winning Contest No. 145, Stanford neuroscientist Patrick House wrote,

> You are not trying to submit the funniest caption; you are trying to win *The New Yorker*'s caption contest. Humor and victory are different matters entirely. . . . Your caption should elicit, at best, a mild chuckle. The first filter for your caption should be: Is it *too* funny? Will it make anyone laugh out loud? If so, throw it out and work on a less funny one.[1]

That's nonsense. But what if you don't have a good sense of humor? Can you learn to be funny? Not according to Jerry Seinfeld, who said, "You can get better at anything you want to get better at—except comedy."[2] Scott Dikkers, a founding editor of *The Onion*, disagrees, especially when it comes to writing.

I met Dikkers at a three-day Comedy Imagination Retreat at the University of Pennsylvania that Mankoff invited me to attend. The last day of this retreat involved a study called "The Neurological Correlates of Creativity in Geniuses." The goal was "to use magnetic resonance imaging to determine the anatomical correlates related to creative thinking in a group of masters/geniuses."[3] In other words, after sitting around for two days talking about humor with other comic geniuses like Scott Dikkers—something Mankoff excels at and enjoys—he would have to spend part of the third day lying still in a coffin-like scanner. Mankoff, who is claustrophobic, wanted me to take the MRI for him, and I liked the idea of pretending to be a genius. No one had ever called me that. No one had even come close.

Dikkers insisted that he had taught people with no sense of humor to become strong comedy writers. That surprised me, and I still question whether someone can learn to be funny. In my opinion, you either have a sense of humor or you don't. But if you have it, you can learn to be really funny. To tweak what Seinfeld said: *You can get better at anything you want to get better at—provided you have a talent for it.*

When Mankoff started the weekly contest in 2005, he said, "I think that a lot of people, if they devoted their lives to this kind of thing, could reliably write funny lines. We'll see if that happens with the more regular contests—if people hone their skills by writing captions more regularly."[4] I don't think you have to devote your life to the contest, but submitting entries every week and participating in the crowdsourcing process (which helps you understand what works and what doesn't and why) will help you improve your caption-writing skills and someday maybe even beat my record.

I'm kidding about that last part. No one will beat my record.

Make Sense

My favorite Robert Leighton cartoon,

*"Can you hang on a sec? I think I just
took another picture of my ear."*

has a backstory:

In 2003, my wife and I were in a restaurant where four girls were waving their phones around. I asked what they were doing, and they explained that their phones had cameras and they were taking pictures. It was the first time I had heard of camera phones. I subsequently learned that you can't photograph your ear with a camera phone because the lens is on the outside. Had I known that, I never would have submitted the cartoon because it makes no sense. Quite often, though, nobody cares.

I care. I just never thought about the placement of the camera lens. Leighton, however, raised an interesting question: Does a successful cartoon have to make sense? In episode 80 of *The New Yorker Cartoon Caption Contest Podcast*, the hosts and their guest, *New Yorker* cartoonist Michael Shaw, addressed that question while discussing the contest that featured this drawing by Sophie Lucido Johnson and Sammi Skolmoski:

Nicole Chrolavicius, of Burlington, Ontario, made it to the finalists' round with, *"He looks ten years less endangered."* Although her entry reconciled the disparate frames of reference—bald eagles, and men who try to look younger by wearing toupees—it didn't actually make sense. You can be less endangered or look ten years younger, but you can't look ten years less endangered.

Shaw said it didn't matter because the caption sounded funny, cartoon logic is not as rigid as regular logic, and one shouldn't overthink cartoon captions. To support his last point he quoted E. B. White: "Humor can be dissected, as a frog can, but the thing dies in the process and the innards are discouraging to any but the pure scientific mind." I didn't think White's admonition applied, and I asked Leighton for his opinion. He said,

> A cartoon should make sense within the parameters that it sets up. Once the reader gets the cartoon, whether that happens instantly or after thinking about the joke, they shouldn't then have a reason to question whether it actually works. I appreciated what the bald eagle caption was going for and, while it didn't make perfect sense, I felt it was a near miss and not fatally flawed.

I like Leighton's "within the parameters" rule. You have to accept the cartoon's premise (for example, that bald eagles can talk and wear toupees). Once you do, however, it's fair to criticize a caption on the grounds that, given the premise, it doesn't make sense.

New Yorker cartoonist Bruce Eric Kaplan addressed that criticism in a *Seinfeld* episode he wrote.[1] Elaine is frustrated because she doesn't understand a *New Yorker* cartoon that's set in an office, where a cat is saying to a dog, "*I've enjoyed reading your email.*" She confronts and demands an explanation from the magazine's cartoon editor, Mr. Elinoff, who at first tries to avoid the subject by saying, "Cartoons are like gossamer, and one doesn't dissect gossamer." Finally, however, he admits that he doesn't get the cartoon and published it only because he "liked the kitty." Elinoff's real-life counterpart, Mankoff, acknowledges that "a few of the *New Yorker* cartoons absolutely have that elusive gossamer quality, where there isn't really this thing that you get. You just sort of enjoy it."[2]

Nicole Chrolavicius, who submitted the bald eagle caption, agrees. "Funny things," she told me, "cause one to *feel* something, rather than to *think* something. If you read a caption and laugh, it is funny and therefore successful. Sometimes the feeling defies explanation, and that's okay."

Elaine would disagree. Irritated by Elinoff's decision to publish a cartoon that made no sense, she says, "You people should be ashamed of yourselves. You doodle a couple of bears at a cocktail party talking about the stock market, you think you're doing comedy." "Actually," Elinoff says, "that's not bad." Flattered, Elaine stays up all night and draws a pig at a complaint department. The pig is saying, "I wish I was taller." Jerry doesn't like that caption and proposes an alternative: "I can't find my receipt. My place is a sty." Kramer suggests, "My wife is a slut." "Now that's a complaint," says Jerry. *The New Yorker* publishes Elaine's cartoon with her caption and she's thrilled until her boss, convinced that he's seen the joke before, investigates and discovers that Elaine subconsciously stole the idea from a *Ziggy* cartoon.

Fourteen years after that *Seinfeld* episode aired, *The New Yorker* assigned Mick

Stevens to redraw Kaplan's cartoon for the caption contest.[3] Here it is, along with the winning caption:

"Stop sending me spam!"
Sean Lynch, Brooklyn, N.Y.

That's not as funny as *"My wife is a slut,"* but it does a nice job of reconciling the disparate elements (pigs and complaint departments) and transforming an ordinary statement into a fitting joke. Elaine would approve.

Make the Speaker Oblivious

Many comedians have built their careers on characters who are blissfully unaware of the obvious. Think of Martin Short as talk show host Jiminy Glick, asking Mel Brooks why he has "such a big beef with the Nazis"; Zach Galifianakis in *Between Two Ferns*, interrupting an interview with Hillary Clinton for a word from the show's sponsor, Donald Trump; and Will Ferrell as anchorman Ron Burgundy, reading from a maliciously-edited teleprompter script and ending both his newscast and career by looking into the camera and saying, "Go fuck yourself, San Diego." Ignorance, stupidity, and willful blindness can be really funny, and some of the best winning captions turn the character who's speaking into what Liz Lemon (Tina Fey's character on *30 Rock*) would call a "certified non-genius":[1]

"Can you please identify which hand was mistakenly amputated?"

Hilary Phillips, Washington, D.C.

Work on Your Delivery

A stand-up comic relies on three things to get a laugh: strong material, facial expressions, and timing. A caption writer doesn't have to worry about expressions—they're in the drawing—but, like the stand-up comic, he needs both a good joke and a strong delivery. The latter comes from writing well. In an interview with Terry Gross, whom he once put in a *New Yorker* cartoon,

"You may have heard me on 'Fresh Air with Terry Gross.' I'm Terry Gross."

David Sipress said, "Every single word, every punctuation mark, everything in the caption matters. You want the reader to glide smoothly through the caption to the punch line without anything distracting them."[1]

Cody Walker understands this. He teaches English at the University of Michigan, and in his classroom he uses the caption contest to dispel the misconception that what you say is all that matters. How you say it is just as important:

Inexperienced writers sometimes imagine that good writing comes from good ideas. But that's not right: good writing comes from good sentences. It comes from caring about sentence construction: the rhythm of the clauses, the placement of the predicate. And working on captions—fiddling with punctuation and modifiers—reinforces this lesson wonderfully. Any sentence that aspires to artfulness—that is, any sentence that you might want to read out loud or share with a friend—makes a kind of gesture. . . . The sentence may raise its (figurative) arms; it may shrug; it may snarl. Whatever the case, it captures an attitude—and it does so efficiently and memorably. Just as good captions do.[2]

Walker won the contest that featured this drawing by P. C. Vey:

"There's a cure—but it's light-years away."
Cody Walker, Ann Arbor, Mich.

Several people submitted essentially the same joke—e.g., "*The good news is that I have a cure for what ails you, the bad news is that it's ten thousand light-years away.*"— but only Walker submitted a good sentence.

By winning the popular vote in a contest featuring a P. C. Vey drawing, Walker succeeded where I have failed three times.

FIRST NEAR-MISS

I made it to the finalists' round by suggesting the shark who's speaking is oblivious ("*Well, that's embarrassing. How long has it been there?*"), but lost to July Kramer, of Broomfield, Colorado, who submitted a line that many teenagers have heard hundreds of times: "*How about some help with the groceries?*"

I became a finalist by making the aliens helpful (*"As long as we're up here, we should do the gutters."*), but Steve Ferguson, of San Rafael, California, won the contest by making them mischievous: *"Can't wait to see the look on his face when we put these back on the tree."*

I made it to the finalists' round by transforming an ordinary statement into a fitting caption: *"I don't usually do this on a first date."* I then lost to Hilton Hebb, of Jacksonville, Florida, who took the same approach: *"You really want to add a kid to all this?"* We both should have lost to Daniel Renton, of Saint John, New Brunswick, who submitted, *"See, I do things around the house."* His solution to a challenging puzzle will resonate with anyone whose partner has made a less than convincing argument that they do their share of household chores. When I saw it in crowd-sourcing I laughed out loud and thought, "There's the winning entry."

I envy Walker his success with a P. C. Vey cartoon, and I can feel that envy curdling into hatred, but his writing advice is sound. To understand its importance, take a look at the winning caption from the contest that featured this drawing by Joe Dator and elicited more than 9,600 submissions:

"I told you we should have salted the roads."
Luke Stancil, Orem, Utah

Now take a look at just three of the more than eight hundred entries that made the same joke, but not nearly as well:

"Yes, I know you said this would happen when we stopped salting the roads."
"This is what happens when you stop salting the roads in winter."
"If you had only salted the streets like I asked you."

It's hard enough to think of a good joke. Don't ruin it with a mediocre delivery.

Choose Your Words Carefully

"The difference between the almost right word and the right word," said Mark Twain, "is the difference between the lightning bug and the lightning." That's especially true in the contest, but does the right word have to be funny? Neil Simon thought so. In his 1972 play, *The Sunshine Boys*, an aging vaudeville comic gives his nephew a lesson in comedy by insisting that words with a hard "k" sound are funny. "Chicken is funny. Pickle is funny. Cab is funny. Cockroach is funny."

The writers of *30 Rock* mocked that advice repeatedly, first by having the inept Dr. Spaceman (pronounced spa-CHE-min) explain that he can't stop giggling while discussing an organ transplant because of the hard "k" sound in kidney.[1] In another episode, Liz complains to her producer Pete that "Jenna accused me of trying to destroy her because her lines don't have any 'k' sounds, which she thinks is the funniest sound." Pete then checks his texts and says, "Oh, my God. My cousin Carl crashed his car, and now he's in a coma at the Kendall Clinic." Meanwhile, Jenna narrowly escapes a falling stage light during a rehearsal of a *Macbeth* sketch and exclaims, "I could have been killed! It's the curse," causing an intern to laugh and then apologize by saying, "Sorry. Hard 'k' sounds."[2]

I don't find words inherently funny. In the context of a particular caption, however, some are definitely funnier than others. Before providing an example, I have to explain something about this Leo Cullum cartoon:

When it appeared in *The New Yorker* as part of the caption contest, the drape was a dark shade of red. Until that point the contest had never featured a color cartoon, and they were a rare sight in the magazine. In fact, the issue with Cullum's drawing included a feature called "What's So Funny About Red?," which was what Harold Ross reportedly said when asked why *The New Yorker* didn't publish cartoons in color.[3]

While looking at Cullum's cartoon, try to imagine the red. It's essential to understanding my winning caption, which is based on the popular misconception that bulls are enraged by that color: "*You should be happy. How many husbands even notice window treatments?*" I doubt I would have won had I ended on the word "drapes" or "curtains" (even with its hard "k" sound). The joke would have been the same, but "window treatments" made it funnier.

Here's another example from David Sipress, who once sent *The New Yorker* a cartoon of a Mayan soccer game: "There's a severed head laying on the ground, and another guy's holding up a regular soccer ball, and the Mayan in charge of the game is saying, 'I don't care if it's bouncier—it threatens the integrity of the game.'" Only after Sipress changed "bouncier" to "more bouncy" did *The New Yorker* buy it.[4]

Sometimes you can get away with a word that is technically incorrect. Here is my winning entry for the contest featuring this drawing by Mick Stevens:

"That explains the signature on the floorboard."
Lawrence Wood, Chicago, Ill.

My friend Kevin, who's an architect, congratulated me by writing, "That's not a floorboard. It's a baseboard."

Eliminate Unnecessary Words

While we're on the subject of words, don't use too many. They can ruin a potentially strong caption. "The real challenge in a contest like this," says Mankoff, "is making [a] general funny idea work in the shortest possible form—using the economy of language and emphasis that's necessary for a good cartoon."[1]

Here's the winning caption from a contest that featured this drawing by Frank Cotham:

"Don't worry, you'll be running in no time."

Tony Bittner, Pittsburgh, Pa.

That came in third out of nearly five thousand entries in crowdsourcing. An almost identical entry—*"Don't worry, you'll be up and running in no time"*—came in 1,221st. How could two little words ("up and") account for such a discrepancy?

There are two reasons. First, the crowdsourcing algorithm can lead to wildly different rankings for nearly identical entries. Once a voter sees a really well-worded caption, they will likely dismiss as "Not Funny" every similar caption that's less well-constructed. The slightly inferior caption then starts appearing less frequently, which means it gets fewer votes overall, and this cycle repeats itself until the caption ends up with a final ranking that's deceptively low. Second, thinking of a good joke isn't enough when other people will likely have the same thought. You must carefully craft the joke and deliver it as well as possible by, among other things, getting rid of every inessential word.

That's how Harry Effron won the contest featuring this drawing by Drew Dernavich:

"The hours here are obscene."
Harry Effron, Briarcliff Manor, N.Y.

Effron subsequently confessed that he could not claim full credit for his entry:

The caption started as my dad's idea, which he submitted. It was, "*The hours here are obscene. Yesterday, I didn't get out until %$*#@.*" Looking back at past contest winners, I realized that the caption was too long. The joke in the first half was enough, so I submitted just that.[2]

Though he stabbed his father in the back, Effron's victory demonstrates the importance of being succinct.

Not every great caption, of course, is short:[3]

"Something's just not right—our air is clean, our water is pure, we all get plenty of exercise, everything we eat is organic and free-range, and yet nobody lives past thirty."

That caption had to be long because the cartoonist, Alex Gregory, was establishing a pattern before ending with something unexpected, and every word was necessary to build the rhythm of the joke before getting to the punch line. Gregory was following the "rule of three" (which he expanded to the rule of four), a comic principle he alluded to in this cartoon:

"You're right—things are funnier in threes."

Here's another rule: long captions are not selected as finalists for the contest. As usual, there are exceptions to this rule:

"*And, when you get hungry, the cafeteria is to your right, left, left, right, left, straight, right, straight, left, and then you push on the big lever.*"

Michael Moran, Evanston, Ill.

But you should try to be concise. Perhaps the best contest-winning caption of all time was a single perfect word:

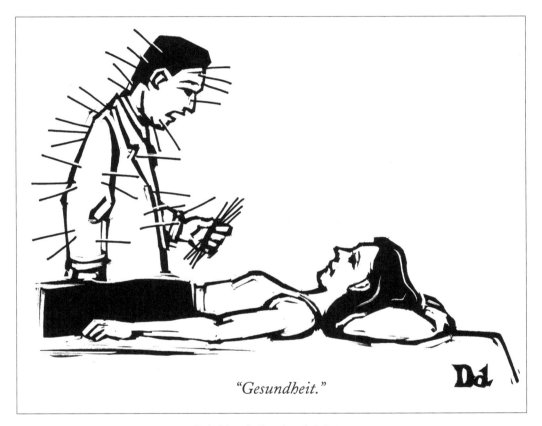

"*Gesundheit.*"

Bob Vogel, Portland, Maine

Punctuate Properly

The New Yorker has exacting standards, and my favorite David Sipress cartoon was initially deemed historically inaccurate:

"I'm having my entrails read."

Sipress told NPR's Terry Gross the story on *Fresh Air*:

I got a note from the fact-checking department that said the knife was incorrectly drawn. It should be a single-bladed knife. . . . and that on the building there were five columns, and there were always only even-numbered columns, so they asked me to change the number of columns. So I wrote back to the fact-checking department, and I said, I understand your problem with the knife. I understand your problem with the number of columns. Why didn't you have a problem with the fact that there's a talking goat?[1]

The New Yorker corrects not only historical inaccuracies but grammatical errors. The commitment to proper grammar can go too far—"sometimes," Mankoff said, "good grammar makes for a very bad cartoon"[2]—but it's usually justified because a missing or misplaced or unnecessary punctuation mark can destroy a joke's rhythm. Before you submit your caption, make sure every period, comma, apostrophe, bracket, parentheses, ellipsis, dash, colon, and semicolon is in the right place. And while we're on the subject of punctuation . . .

No Exclamation Points!

You should use an exclamation point only when your caption is an actual exclamation: "Fire!" or "Help!" or "You're a *Jew*, for Christ's sake!"—something my father yelled at me after I came home drunk during my senior year of high school.

Sometimes the winning entry uses an exclamation point to perfect effect:

"Objection, Your Honor! Alleged killer whale."

Will Simon, Brooklyn, N.Y.

Most of the time, however, exclamation points are unnecessary. Still, they appear with surprising frequency in the caption contest. A random sample of twenty consecutive contests revealed that the average number of entries that ended with an exclamation point was more than 1,300 (approximately 20 percent of the total).

What accounts for the indiscriminate use of the exclamation point? Emails and texts. In a *New York Times* article, Aimee Lee Bell noted, "Writing is by definition an imperfect medium for relaying the human voice. And in the age of electronic communication, when that voice is transmitted so often via email and text message, many literate and articulate people find themselves justifying the exclamation point to convey emotion, enthusiasm, or excitement."[1] Ironically, all the well-intentioned efforts to convey feeling have only desensitized us:

"I've grown numb to exclamation points."

Some defenders of the exclamation point claim that "attempts to condemn the mark smack of a dog whistle for sexism."[2] The idea is that women use the exclamation point more than men—"the writer Amelia Tait calls it 'emotional labor' in grammatical form, shouldering the responsibility to ease tension or hurt"[3]—and attempts to denigrate its use are just the latest in a long line of patriarchal or even misogynistic efforts to belittle feminine forms of expression. Donald Trump would agree. He loves the exclamation point—more than half his tweets end with one[4]—and he sees himself as a historically strong proponent of women's rights. On August 14, 2020, he tweeted: "I have done more for WOMEN than just about any President in HISTORY!"

Using an exclamation point is almost never a good idea. In an episode of *Seinfeld*,[5] Elaine, an assistant book editor, breaks up with her writer boyfriend because he did not use an exclamation point when leaving a note about her friend who just had a baby. Elaine then edits his manuscript by replacing many of the periods with exclamation points. Her boss, Mr. Lippman, calls her into his office:

LIPPMAN: I was just reading your final edit and there seems to be an inordinate number of exclamation points.

ELAINE: Well, I thought the writing lacked a certain emotion and intensity.

LIPPMAN: Ahhh. "It was a damp and chilly afternoon so I decided to put on . . . my sweatshirt!" You put an exclamation point after "sweatshirt."

ELAINE: That's correct. Well, I felt that the character didn't like to be chilly.

LIPPMAN: I see. "I pulled the lever on the machine but the Clark bar didn't . . . come out!" Exclamation point.

ELAINE: Well, you know how frustrating that can be when you keep putting quarters and quarters into a machine and then nothing comes out.

LIPPMAN: Get . . . rid . . . of the exclamation points. I *hate* exclamation points.

So do I, and so does Mike Twohy's cat:

"You tend to overuse the exclamation point."

Don't Bury the Punch Line

Your caption should end with the punch line—the word or phrase that surprises the reader and gives the cartoon meaning. Putting the punch line in the middle of your caption dilutes the impact of your joke.

When Drew Dernavich, a *New Yorker* cartoonist whose work often appears in the contest, participates in crowdsourcing to see how people are captioning his work, his inner critic comes out. "I want to write to everybody and provide feedback," he says, "especially if they bury the punch line. Put it at the end! Not the middle!"

Alex Gregory agrees. He was a staff cartoonist for *The New Yorker,* and he is an Emmy-winning screenwriter whose television credits include *King of the Hill, The Larry Sanders Show,* and *Veep.* "Writing comedy and creating strong captions," he says, "both depend on putting the twist at the end or as late in the sentence as possible."

There were more than 6,500 entries for the contest that featured this cartoon by Ed Koren:

Someone submitted a decent pandemic joke—"*Maybe these are the novel variants they're talking about.*"—but buried the punch line, which was "novel variants." The winning caption from Randall Beren, of San Rafael, California, put the punch line at the end, where it belonged: "*The classics can be so intimidating.*" There are actually two potential punch lines in that caption—intimidating and classics—and another entry that did well in crowdsourcing (coming in only four spots behind the winner) went with the second option: "*I've always been intimidated by the classics.*"

Don't Be Too Predictable

won my first caption contest on April 30, 2007:

"If he's so damn intelligent, let him get a job."

Lawrence Wood, Chicago, Ill.

A colleague told me my entry was good but obvious. "Anyone looking at that drawing," she said, "would have come up with that line." Her backhanded compliment was actually high praise. The best captions appear obvious once you've seen them, but are hard to think of when you're staring at a captionless drawing.

Some captions, however, really *are* too predictable, and you should resist the urge to submit one that springs to mind immediately. There are exceptions to this rule, as inspiration can strike quickly. Contest-winner Cary Wong said, "I usually go with whatever hits me when I see the picture."[1] That strategy worked for him in the contest featuring this drawing by Danny Shanahan:

"Wait. Would we still be doing this if the sky weren't falling?"

Cary Wong, New York City

In general, though, you should wait awhile and give yourself a chance to dig deeper. Consider what film director and comedian Adam McKay said he learned from his improv coach, Del Close: "When you're onstage, your first thought is knee-jerk. Your second thought is usually okay, but not great. Del would make you stay in a scene until you found your third thought, which was a little above and beyond what most other teachers would suggest."[2] This approach works not only for improv comedy, but for the contest.

Here's another reason to resist your first idea: if it's obvious to you, it will be obvious to hundreds of people you're competing against, which means your entry will likely get lost in the sea of similar or even identical submissions. Mankoff warned against "writing the most predictable caption. If ten thousand people enter, and three hundred of them write almost the exact same line . . . it's very unlikely that will be the winning caption. . . . The most predictable formulations, while they might make a perfectly serviceable caption, aren't likely to win."[3]

The contest that featured this drawing by Shannon Wheeler

elicited more than 1,500 references to either "Stayin' Alive" or "I Will Survive," and nearly seven hundred dance fever jokes. There is, of course, one advantage to submitting such an obvious caption. If you beat the formidable odds and make it to the finalists' round, you have a good shot at winning the contest because the hundreds of entrants who submitted the same joke will be inclined to vote for you. That may be why Paul Greenwood, of Pickering, Ontario, won the contest featuring Shannon Wheeler's drawing with, "*The patient has requested 'Stayin' Alive.'*"

Don't Be Too Unpredictable

W hen it comes to funny," Mankoff says, "novelty is overrated."

In a 1974 experiment, subjects listened to recordings of Bill Cosby and Phyllis Diller stand-up routines. For one group of subjects the tape was stopped just before the punch lines, and they were asked to predict them. The other subjects listened straight through and rated the jokes. The more predictable punch lines were rated as funnier.[1]

Does that mean you should ignore all my prior advice about avoiding obvious jokes? No. You should strike a balance between jokes that are too predictable and those that are so surprising they won't resonate with most readers. When someone sees your caption, you don't want them to say, "What?" Nor do you want them to roll their eyes and think, "Obviously." You want them to wonder, "Why didn't I think of that?"

Don't Get Cute

Colloquialisms have their place—"Musta Notta Gotta Lotta" is a great title for Joe Ely's hard-driving rockabilly song, and much better than "Must Have Not Have Gotten a Lot Of"—but they don't work in captions. They come across as cute, and I hate cute humor. I don't hate it as much as Michael O'Donoghue did—he was the first head writer for *Saturday Night Live*, and he said that humor is not about a kitten tangled in a ball of string unless the kitten gets strangled[1]—but it irritates me.

Nevertheless, some contest-winning captions have included colloquialisms:

"You shoulda heard the mockingbirds this morning."
Jack Visser, Troy, N.Y.

I suspect Visser was trying to capture the way people actually talk, but "shoulda" is a distracting word that adds nothing to an otherwise fine joke.

Think of Many Captions

The New Yorker selects three finalists for every contest because there is always more than one good way to caption a drawing. Staff cartoonist Robert Leighton loves this aspect of the contest. "I really enjoy looking at the finalists that have been selected for other artists' cartoons," he said, "especially when I've been captivated by the drawing and thought about what I might do with it. When I see three finalists and each one approaches the cartoon from a different angle, I find that inspirational."

The almost limitless captioning possibilities became apparent during *The New Yorker*'s first annual contest, which, as noted previously, featured this drawing by Jack Ziegler:

The winning entry came from Vince Banes, of Silver Spring, Maryland: *"Mom, Dad's been on eBay again!"* *The New Yorker* then highlighted an additional seventeen entries and organized them by category—alcohol, antitrust, books, domestic life, environmentalism, language, local all-news radio, Malthusianism (the theory that population growth is exponential and must be controlled so it does not outpace agricultural growth and trigger a catastrophe), medication, mythology-based homonyms, objectivism, psychiatry, sarcasm, sex, shopping, sports, and understatement.[1]

Even if you can't think of a good Malthusianism joke—my favorite is comedian Bill Burr's proposed solution to the population crisis: "Look, 85 percent of you have to go."—try to come up with as many ideas as possible. Keith Sawyer supports this strategy. He is the Morgan Distinguished Professor of Educational Innovations at the University of North Carolina at Chapel Hill, and a psychologist who studies the creative process.

> Cartoon contest winners usually generate lots of captions. Studies of creativity have shown that quantity breeds quality—what I call the *productivity theory*, because high productivity corresponds to high creativity. When the famous physicist Freeman Dyson was asked how to generate good ideas, he said, "Have a lot of ideas, then throw out the bad ones." Cartoon caption winners are no different.[2]

I may not generate lots of captions for every contest, but I come up with at least three. Here are a few examples:

"After clawing the hell out of this couch, you're worried about staining it?"
"Really? I love torturing mice, too."
"It pairs nicely with dead mice."

"It's twelve million dollars, but alterations are free."

"Don't worry. The fabric's not breathable."

"Is the suit for work?"

"*He symbolizes the worst of America.*"
"*He's struggling with turning ten.*"
"*He uses every part of the rodent.*"

Get Help

If your friends are funny, let them review your captions before you decide which one to submit. They may hate them all—my friends often do. Consider their opinions carefully, but don't hesitate to reject their recommendations if you think they're wrong. I learned that lesson the hard way while trying to decide which of the following three captions to submit for the contest featuring this drawing by Frank Cotham:

"Dress for the job you have."
"You might want to loosen your tie."
"No one told you about casual Friday?"

I liked my first caption, but my friends didn't. Then Rita K. Lomio, of Washington, D.C., became a finalist with the exact same caption, word for word, that my friends had rejected. Congratulations, Rita. I wish I had your friends. (Rita lost the popular vote to Nick Kanellis, of Brooklyn, New York, who submitted, *"Your last job sounds terrible,"* a wonderful line that deserved the top spot.)

Don't Recycle

Two of the captions I considered for the Frank Cotham cartoon—*"Dress for the job you have,"* and *"No one told you about casual Friday?"*—were fine at the time, but have in the years since become stale caption clichés. They need to be retired, as do all variations on the "bigger boat" line from *Jaws*:

"We're gonna need a bigger spear."

Peter Lorber, Thousand Oaks, Calif.

"We're gonna need a bigger cat."

Jeff Burd, Gurnee, Ill.

Contest No. 853 featured a Sam Marlow cartoon that seemed to beg for a third version of the same joke, so my entry encouraged the judges to go in another direction:

"I guess I should say 'We're gonna need a bigger board,' but some variation on the 'bigger boat' line from Jaws *has made it to the finalists' round in two other contests and enough's enough."*

I don't often submit captions that have the characters acknowledging they're in a cartoon. Meta humor can be great—in *Monty Python's Flying Circus*, characters routinely broke the fourth wall to comment on the fact that they were in a sketch—but it rarely works in the contest. There are exceptions to this rule—the Mick Stevens cartoon I captioned with, "*That explains the signature on the floorboard*" demanded a meta joke—but in general you should avoid self-referential humor.

As I suspected, "*We're gonna need a bigger board*" was Marlow's original caption—I spoke to him after the contest ended—and it did well in crowdsourcing, coming in sixth place out of almost five thousand entries. Fortunately, the judges did not select it as a finalist. Although it's a fitting caption for a great drawing, any reference to the "bigger boat" line is by now well past its expiration date.

Here are ten more of the most frequently recycled captions—they appear all the time in crowdsourcing—and I hope to never see any of them again.

"*Where do you see yourself in [however many days or years]?*"
"*I'm here to talk to you about your car's extended warranty.*"
"*You don't understand the gravity of the situation.*"
"*You don't look like your profile picture.*"
"*It's an emotional support animal.*"
"*The drugs are kicking in.*"
"*It no longer sparks joy.*"
"*I'm working remotely.*"
"*My eyes are up here.*"
"*It's mostly water weight.*"

That last entry was selected as a finalist in no fewer than three contests, and in two of them it was submitted by the very same person (Vin Coca, who co-hosts the caption contest podcast):

"It's mostly water weight."
Vincent Coca, Staten Island, N.Y.

"It's mostly water weight."
Vincent Coca, Staten Island, N.Y.

"It's mostly water weight."
Derek Simmonsen, Baltimore, Md.

The New Yorker came very close to choosing another recycled caption as a finalist for Contest No. 849, which featured this drawing by Kaamran Hafeez:

Michael Moran, who, you may remember, won the contest featuring Navied Mahdavian's drawing of a research scientist addressing her new colleague (a human-size mouse wearing a lab coat), submitted the exact same caption for the Hafeez cartoon. His strategy worked, at least for a while. On June 1, 2023, *The New Yorker* notified him that his entry had been selected as a finalist. The next day, however, associate cartoon editor Rachel Perlman wrote, "After further research, we are pulling your caption because you've already won with it before on a cartoon with a similar setup."

Apparently, therefore, *The New Yorker* rejects a recycled caption only if it's been used for a similar scenario, but I wish there were a complete ban on such entries. The point of the contest is not to take a caption that's already been featured and see whether it works in another context; it's to come up with an original idea.

Don't Get Discouraged

Most of the time your caption won't be selected as a finalist. When I started entering the contest, I was disappointed on a weekly basis for almost two years. Here are a couple of my captions from that period that didn't make the cut:

"This is what comes of turning water into wine."

"*Yeah, I'm the reason you feel trapped.*"

Roger Ebert knew how that felt. In 2009, he wrote on his *Chicago Sun-Times* blog:

I have entered the *New Yorker*'s Cartoon Caption Contest almost weekly since it
began and have never even been a finalist. Mark Twain advised: "Write without pay
until somebody offers to pay you. If nobody offers within three years, sawing wood
is what you were intended for." I have done more writing for free for the *New Yorker*
in the last five years than for anybody in the previous 40 years.

  It's not that I think my cartoon captions are better than anyone else's, although
some weeks, understandably, I do. It's just that once I want to see one of my damn
captions in the magazine that publishes the best cartoons in the world.[1]

After more than one hundred unsuccessful attempts, Ebert finally achieved his
goal by winning the contest that featured this drawing by Tom Cheney:

"*I'm not going to say the word I'm thinking of.*"

Roger Ebert, Chicago, Ill.

The Atlantic suggested that Ebert's fame may have prevented him from winning sooner.

Mankoff has previously put the odds of winning the contest at 10,000:1, which makes Chicago attorney Larry Wood's record four wins all the more impressive. But Wood is a rank-and-file lawyer for a nonprofit legal aid organization, and Ebert is a famous media personality. It would never do for the publication to start handing awards to an outsize number of famous people. Even though Mankoff didn't say it, that's probably part of why it took Ebert this long to win. If average readers start thinking they have to be Roger Ebert in order to win, they'll stop submitting.[2]

In a newspaper article announcing his victory, Ebert wrote, "I have not yet begun to fight. A Chicago man, Lawrence Wood, is the *New Yorker* cartoon contest's world champion with four wins. I'm coming for you, Wood."[3] Ebert tried to make good on that threat, entering all but one of the next ninety-three contests before passing away on April 4, 2013.

Don't Be Vulgar

The day after Roger Ebert died, Mankoff honored him by highlighting some of his best contest entries, including this one[1]:

"Now watch how I lift my tray table to its original and upright position."

That is an outstanding caption. Unfortunately, it's also an erection joke, and jokes like that don't appear in the contest. They appear in *The Rejection Collection: Cartoons You Never Saw, and Never Will See, in The New Yorker*, edited by *New Yorker* cartoonist Matthew Diffee.

I was tempted to submit a vulgar caption only once, when the contest featured this drawing by Liam Francis Walsh:

Because of the shape of the microphone, I considered, "*Thanks for letting me use your vibrator.*" I chickened out, though, and went with a much less explicit sex joke: "*You draw the line at faking a laugh?*"

The New Yorker's cartoon department isn't prudish. Several caption contests have featured nudity:

"*First, I'd like to thank the podium.*"

Brendan Hasenstab, Brooklyn, N.Y.

"And what does she have that I don't?"

Christo Phillips, Brooklyn, N.Y.

One even had a sex doll:

"*Hey, you teach CPR your way and I'll teach it mine.*"
Rose Locander, Waukesha, Wis.

Nevertheless, there is a line that must never be crossed, and Ebert leapt over it with his joke about an airline passenger's surprisingly powerful erection. So toe the line. If you're submitting a sex joke, make sure it's not vulgar. And don't include in your caption the kind of strong profanity you might see in other parts of the magazine. The standards are different.

Mary Norris, a proofreader at the magazine for twenty-four years, wrote that there was an informal competition among the writers to see who "could get the most instances of 'fuck' into print."[2] John McPhee used the expletive fourteen times in a single paragraph, which he began with, "Fuck, fucker, fuckest; fuckest, fucker, fuck."[3] He may have been inspired by Ian Frazier's "Cursing Mommy," whose profanity-laced tirades ("Please don't fucking tell me the Rose's Lime Juice is not fucking here."[4]) were featured in a series of "Shouts and Murmurs" pieces. And film critic Anthony Lane used the word to great effect in his withering review of *Star Wars: Episode III—Revenge of the Sith*, when he mocked Yoda's "screwy syntax" by writing, "Break me a fucking give."[5] But you will never see that kind of language in the contest. When Zachary Kanin worked in *The New Yorker*'s cartoon department and reviewed a total of 470,608 contest entries,[6] he eliminated every one that included the word "fuck."[7]

Don't Be Shocking

In 1925, when it made its debut, *The New Yorker* was a humor magazine. "There are early issues," wrote Joshua Rothman, the ideas editor for newyorker.com, "in which nearly every article is funny."[1] Another humor magazine, *National Lampoon*, made its debut forty-five years later, but the two publications had little in common.

The New Yorker's humor was sophisticated—it complemented the magazine's acclaimed fiction, essays, journalism, and criticism—while the *Lampoon*'s was profane and defiant, gleefully violating taboos and attacking whatever was considered sacred. These differences were reflected in the cartoons each magazine published, even when the cartoons came from the same artist.

Both magazines published Sam Gross's cartoons, but his work for *The New Yorker* was charming—a snail declaring his love for a tape dispenser; a bull telling a calf that his mother, who's jumping over the moon, "is a remarkable woman"; an airborne penguin explaining to other penguins why he can suddenly fly (*"We just haven't been flapping them hard enough."*). By contrast, his work for *National Lampoon*, where he was, for some years, the cartoon editor, prompted the cartoonist John Callahan to call him "the granddaddy of the sick cartoon."[2] This one appeared on the cover of *National Lampoon*'s 1977 comedy album, *That's Not Funny, That's Sick!*

When you're entering the caption contest, try to be like the *New Yorker* version of Sam Gross. I went in the other direction only once, when Contest No. 855 featured this cartoon by Liza Donnelly:

Because there were no children in the drawing, I suggested they had been killed by a car speeding through the house: "*Sure, I miss the kids, but we told them to look both ways.*" I knew that was pushing the limit, so after submitting the caption I sent it to Liza's husband, *New Yorker* cartoonist Michael Maslin, for his opinion. He wrote back, "Too bad *National Lampoon* isn't still around (and hosting a caption contest). A sure winner for them."

Get Out the Vote

If *The New Yorker* selects your caption as a finalist, you must then win the popular vote. You could sit back and do nothing, confident that readers will recognize the merits of your entry and vote accordingly, but I don't recommend that approach. Beg everyone you know for their support.

After I won my third contest, *Time* interviewed me and asked, "Once you become a finalist, do you wage a guerrilla campaign to get the vote out?" "Oh, an aggressive one," I said.

I'll email everyone in my agency, which has about 200 people. I'm careful to delete from that email group the two or three people that I know hate me, because I don't want them to launch some kind of counter-offensive. I'll email my friends. They'll email some of their friends. I don't know how far and wide that goes, but I email the people I'm in regular contact with. I think you have to do that; I think every finalist does.[1]

Years later my friend Neha criticized this system as inefficient. "Email was fine back when you started winning these contests," she said, "but no one uses it anymore. Have your daughters show you how to get on Instagram." My reliance on email and refusal to use social media may explain why I won the popular vote seven times prior to 2016, and only once thereafter despite having made it to the finalists' round an additional seven times.

Another possible explanation is that no one wants me to win anymore. "Enough's enough," said my friend Mary. "Move on to something else." Mary also told me to take down the framed prints of my winning captions from a wall in my living room. "It's a living room," she said. "Not a shrine."

Summing Up

That was a lot of advice, so here it is in short form for easy reference:

1. Correctly identify the character who's delivering the line that will serve as your caption.

2. Make sure you know what's happening in the cartoon. Don't mistake lemons for scones.

3. Make your caption consistent with the expression of every character in the drawing. If a smiling pumpkin is speaking to a roomful of worried-looking pumpkins, your caption should acknowledge and make sense of the different expressions.

4. Address every important aspect of the cartoon. If a dog and cat appear in the drawing, comment on their relationship.

5. Every so often, try focusing on a seemingly insignificant detail.

6. Don't just describe what's happening in the cartoon. Tell a story.

7. Put yourself in the story. What would you say if you were the character who's speaking?

8. Consider transforming an ordinary statement into something that takes on an entirely new and humorous meaning within the context of the cartoon.

9. If you're struggling to think of a caption, make a list that helps you reconcile the cartoon's disparate frames of reference.

10. Don't settle for being clever. Be funny.

11. Accept the premise of the cartoon, no matter how outlandish, but ensure that your caption makes sense within the parameters of this premise.

12. Try making the speaker oblivious.

13. Work on your delivery.

14. Choose your words carefully.

15. Eliminate unnecessary words. Your caption doesn't have to be short (though the best ones often are), but it must be well-constructed. If a word doesn't have to be in your caption, delete it.

16. Punctuate properly. A lazy mistake can affect the rhythm of your joke.

17. Avoid unnecessary exclamation points, and they're almost always unnecessary. As Mankoff once noted, "Shouting a joke doesn't make it any funnier, except to a deaf person."[1]

18. Put the punch line where it belongs, at the end of your caption.

19. Don't be too obvious. Go for your "third thought," which will likely be funnier than your first and different from the thousands of entries you're competing against.

20. On the other hand, don't be too unpredictable. You're not going to win the contest by confusing people.

21. Don't use colloquialisms like "gonna" and "shoulda."

22. Think of many captions, and then select the best.
23. Ask your friends to help you make this selection.
24. Don't recycle lines that have become tired caption clichés. Don't even think about submitting three-time finalist, "*It's mostly water weight.*"
25. Persevere. It's hard to win the contest, and easy to get discouraged when you repeatedly fail to make the finalists' round, but keep at it. Be like Roger Ebert, who entered more than one hundred times before finally grabbing the brass ring.
26. Don't be vulgar. I love inappropriate jokes, but there's a difference between the caption contest and Matt Diffee's *The Rejection Collection.*
27. Don't be shocking. You're trying to get in *The New Yorker*, not *National Lampoon.*
28. If your caption is selected as a finalist, launch an aggressive social media campaign to win the popular vote. Don't rely solely on email to drum up support for your entry.
29. Never lend anything of value to a University of Chicago student.

Some of my suggestions (avoid unnecessary explanation points) are easier to follow than others (be funny), but if you heed my advice you will be that much closer to seeing your name in *The New Yorker.*

WINNING ISN'T EVERYTHING

I have no more advice on how to improve your chances of becoming a finalist, but I still have a lot to say about the contest, which is a surprisingly controversial subject. Some cartoonists, including a few whose drawings appear regularly in the contest, dismiss the winning entries as clever at best. That's a fair criticism of some winning captions, but I will argue that a good number are just as funny, if not as meaningful, as regular *New Yorker* cartoons. I was relieved to learn that many *New Yorker* cartoonists agree.

In the early days, *The New Yorker* encouraged its cartoonists to collaborate with writers—the magazine subsequently discouraged the practice before again changing its position—and I will consider whether the contest represents such a collaboration. Even if it doesn't, the contest demonstrates that terrific cartoons are not always the result of a single vision.

I have collaborated with four *New Yorker* cartoonists, and I will highlight some of our joint efforts while bragging that I lost my most lucrative captioning job to a famous comedian. I will then examine what the contest can teach us about parallel thinking, the subjectivity of humor, anti-humor, and the problem with puns. I will also commiserate with a few of the many contest participants who did not receive the recognition they deserved for their excellent entries. Finally, I'll explain how data from the contest is helping scientists who are trying to improve artificial intelligence programs. So if your interest in the contest extends beyond learning how to win it, keep reading.

The Great Debate

In 2014, *New Yorker* cartoonist Kaamran Hafeez ran a caption contest on his website and tried to sell the completed cartoons to the magazine. I won four of the contests, including the two that featured these drawings:

"He's very detail oriented."

"Never insult housekeeping."

Unfortunately, none of my (and none of the other) winning captions led to a published cartoon in *The New Yorker*. Hafeez therefore abandoned his experiment and, in the process, dismissed the magazine's contest as a gimmick that generates clever—but not funny—captions. "The results," he contended, "rarely, if ever, rise to the level of actual *New Yorker* cartoons. The winners of caption contests come off as very clever responses to the drawing—nothing more."

When I asked Lars Kenseth, a *New Yorker* cartoonist and TV writer whose credits include *Chuck Deuce* and *Norm Macdonald Has a Show*, whether he thought the contest-winning entries were funny or merely clever, he said, "I just went through twenty recent winners and laughed quite a bit. If I had to ballpark it, I'd say they're 60 percent funny, 40 percent clever."

New Yorker cartoonist Sophie Lucido Johnson rejects the distinction and thinks we do a disservice to contest-winning captions by dismissing them as nothing more than clever solutions. "Comedy," she says, "is *so often* about finding such solutions. It's not an easy thing to do! Being funny can be easy; puzzle-solving can be difficult. In any case, I do think the captions are funny."

Mick Stevens, whose drawings have been featured in the contest more than fifty times, thinks she's wrong. "I'd say the contest has lowered the bar when it comes to humor. It suggests that anyone can be funny, then proves that's not so." Alex Gregory disagrees. "The contest," he said, "shows that humor is more universal and democratic than one might think. If my cartoons had never been published in the magazine, I likely would have obsessed over the contest. I know some of my fellow cartoonists were not fans, and I can only guess that it was threatening to see non-cartoonists write captions as well as they could."

Robert Leighton said, "The winning captions and runners-up are often very funny, but when they exist only to justify the drawing, they result in cartoons *The New Yorker* likely wouldn't have bought." To illustrate the difference between captions that "work" and those that go a step further and create truly outstanding cartoons, he compared two winning entries:

"Listen to this baby purr."
Broderick Goodnight, Kokomo, Ind.

"I only knew about the moral code."
Susan Sturm, Springfield, Ill.

The first, Leighton said, "solves Tom Toro's puzzle by addressing both the cat and luxury cars, but what does the completed cartoon mean? What is it about? Nothing but its own cleverness." By contrast, Leighton said, the second caption is brilliant, as it suggests that multicolored "Go to Hell" pants (part of a preppy fashion movement that rebelled against the more conservative clothing favored by

Madison Avenue types) violate even the most forgiving dress codes. "Not only is it a clever and funny solution to Michael Shaw's puzzle; it's thought-provoking. There's a moral code that governs life, but is there some other requirement (maybe even a bigger one) that we don't know about?"

Drew Dernavich said that many winning captions are clever as opposed to funny because of the very nature of the contest.

> There are two ways to create a cartoon—by starting with the joke, or by starting with the image. If you start with a joke, and the joke is good, your cartoon will be funny. If you start with the image and then try to come up with a caption that makes sense of that image—which is what everybody who enters the contest is trying to do—your caption will likely be clever but not necessarily funny.

Nevertheless, he said, a good number of the contest-winning captions are both clever *and* funny. "But even the best," he continued, "are not meaningful, and that's where they fall short. My favorite cartoons do two things: they elicit a laugh, and they provide insight. It's not easy to create such cartoons—it's hard to be funny *and* profound—but that's always my goal."

It's a laudable goal, but the winning entries in the caption contest aren't meant to be profound. They're solutions to a comic puzzle, and many are genuinely funny. Despite what Hafeez initially thought (he subsequently changed his mind), a good number of contest-winning cartoons can hold their own against the funniest *New Yorker* cartoons. Here is a small but representative sample:

"*Are you now, or have you ever been?*"

Stuart Spitalnic, Saunderstown, R.I.

"Tap is fine."

Lauren Waits, Atlanta, Ga.

"Yeah, yeah—and I invented the ticket."

Scott Gerschwer, Redding, Conn.

"Hold on, *the Senate Committee on Women's Health is getting out.*"

Chris Jannsen, San Jose, Calif.

"Until I recover, let's just assume your prostate is fine."

Jeff Goodman, Burnsville, N.C.

Two Heads Are (Sometimes) Better Than One

Keith Sawyer, the psychologist I quoted earlier on the importance of coming up with as many captions as possible, wrote that "everyone who enters the caption contest is collaborating with the cartoonist. The cartoonist launches the contest by generating an ambiguous cartoon, one that can be interpreted many different ways. This kind of ambiguity, the kind that opens up many future possibilities, often prompts innovation."[1]

Some *New Yorker* cartoonists reject Sawyer's premise. "The contest is not a collaboration," said Michael Maslin, a frequent contributor to the magazine and the creator of *Ink Spill*, a website devoted to *New Yorker* cartoons and cartoonists:

> If I served you eggs for breakfast and you added some Tabasco sauce, we did not collaborate on the making of the eggs. When I submit a captionless drawing to the magazine and it ends up in the contest, it's like a puzzle I couldn't solve and I'm curious to see what others do with it. But when *The New Yorker* removes my caption from a cartoon I submitted and uses the drawing for the contest, it feels like the magazine took a puzzle I *had* solved and turned it into something else entirely: a game for its readers. And that's fine, but in neither situation am I participating in a collaborative process.

New Yorker cartoonist Peter Kuper agrees. "There's no collaboration, especially since I have no role in selecting the finalists. I just stand back and watch as the captions take my drawing in a direction I did not anticipate."

It's hard to argue with Maslin and Kuper on this point, but it may not matter. Even if the contest is not an example of true collaboration, it can lead to the creation of something unexpectedly good and maybe even better than anything the cartoonist had imagined. Alex Gregory singled out the following winning entry as "chef's kiss perfect and better than any caption I had in mind."

"Fine. If it's a boy, we'll call him Boy. But if it's a girl, I want to call her McKenzie."
Fairleigh Brooks, Louisville, Ky.

Christopher Weyant thinks most of the winning entries from contests that feature his drawings are not as strong as his original captions. "My writing is pretty specific and personal so it's hard to break up the cartoon into parts and have it work better." Nevertheless, he cited the following entry as a notable exception to the rule:

"Remember back when the worst thing you could catch around here was athlete's foot?"

Charles Beckman, Towson, Md.

"I struggled for ages to come up with a good caption for that drawing, trying different approaches and resubmitting ideas unsuccessfully. The winning entry was exactly what my cartoon needed. Just great."

John Klossner said that some winning captions were much better than his original ideas:

"No, you come in on four."
Colin Mills, Boston, Mass.

Others were good but not significantly better:

"I'm always afraid he will drop in unexpectedly."
Dan Rose, San Francisco, Calif.

And a few were "meh." He didn't include mine in that category, but he probably should have:

"It's only fair. He has a man cave."
Lawrence Wood, Chicago, Ill.

That's not my best work, but here are a couple of my winning captions that were, I think, better than the cartoonists' original ideas:

"*Both the movie and I will be released this summer.*"

Lawrence Wood, Chicago, Ill.

Jack Ziegler's original caption—"*I love what you've done since that last home invasion.*"—addressed the bars on the window but not the talk show setting.

"It's unplugged. I'm not an idiot."

Lawrence Wood, Chicago, Ill.

Tom Cheney's original line ("*Believe me—I regretted it the moment I drove it off the lot.*") suggests that the man actually drives the toaster and defies even cartoon logic.

New Yorker cartoonist Ellis Rosen is on the fence when it comes to the comparative merits of his original ideas and the winning captions. "On several occasions," he said, "I really liked my caption, but I could see why it didn't work as well as the contest-winner." Here's the winning entry from a contest that featured one of his drawings:

"*Of course—we wait forever, then two come at the same time.*"
Elizabeth Novick, Brooklyn, N.Y.

"That's better," said Rosen, "than my original idea, which was just too weird: '*They're peaceful, but stand clear of their closing doors.*'" Rosen's not willing, however, to admit the superiority of this entry:

"*I told your parents I would convert.*"
Catherine Jacobs, New York City

"My original line was very similar: '*I must, Lucille. It's the only way your father will let us marry.*' The winning caption is snappier than mine, so I can understand why some people prefer it, but I still like my version. I like the name Lucille and the melodramatic language, which sets the scene and builds a richer narrative."

No matter how the winning entries compare to the cartoonists' original captions, the contest is part of *The New Yorker*'s long tradition of pairing artists with gag writers.

Collaborating at *The New Yorker*

In the magazine's early days, fiction editor Katharine White helped Harold Ross review cartoon submissions at the weekly art meetings. The writer William Maxwell, who started his long tenure at *The New Yorker* by serving as White's assistant, recalled that "occasionally, Mrs. White would say that the picture might be saved if it had a better caption, and it would be returned to the artist or sent to E. B. White, who was a whiz at this."[1] E. B. White's most famous contribution (a now rare example of a caption with multicharacter dialogue) appeared beneath Carl Rose's drawing of a mother coaxing her daughter to eat vegetables. The mother says, "*It's broccoli, dear,*" and her daughter replies, "*I say it's spinach, and I say the hell with it.*"[2]

Ross saw nothing wrong with such collaborations. "So help me," he wrote, "there's no sin, no harm, and nothing unethical in drawing up an idea suggested by a man who can't possibly draw it himself."[3] Sometimes the idea man could draw quite well. *New Yorker* cartoonist John Ruge, for example, provided the caption for this Peter Arno classic:[4]

"Well, back to the old drawing board."

In the process, Ruge coined an expression that entered the lexicon and is now used by millions of people who don't know its origin.

Legendary cartoonists like George Price and Helen Hokinson regularly used gag writers. Price, in fact, relied on them exclusively, never writing his own captions, and Hokinson collaborated for eighteen years with the writer James Reid Parker. James Geraghty, the magazine's art editor from 1939 to 1973, was not himself an artist. He started out as a freelance "idea man," selling concepts to *New Yorker* cartoonists like Peter Arno, Richard Decker, Barney Tobey, and Perry Barlow, and for more than three decades he continued to provide gags for the cartoonists.[5]

In 1947, the novelist Peter De Vries, who was contributing short fiction to the magazine and writing for the "Notes and Comment" section, asked Geraghty if there was anything he could do in the Art Department.[6] Geraghty put him to work "part time as a cartoon doctor, improving captions and finding gags for artists."[7] De Vries's experience as an idea man likely inspired his 1954 novel, *The Tunnel of Love*, about a gag writer at a magazine very much like *The New Yorker* who yearns to be a cartoonist.

In 1973, when Lee Lorenz succeeded Geraghty as art editor, the Cartoon Department adopted a new approach and started requiring the artists to come up with their own captions. Reflecting on the change years later, Lorenz said, "Of course there was a long tradition [at *The New Yorker*] of people who just did the ideas and the artists who just did the drawings, but we'd gotten past that."[8] The Frank Sinatra model of performing someone else's material was out, and the singer-songwriter model exemplified by Bob Dylan was in.

Cartoonists like Michael Maslin and Roz Chast, who likened the use of outside help to cheating,[9] welcomed the change. When I asked Maslin whether he had ever collaborated with a gag writer, he said, "Never have. Never will. It's unthinkable." Many years ago, however, he unwittingly assumed the role of an idea man when he submitted two cartoons to *The New Yorker* and the magazine bought just his concepts, giving one to Whitney Darrow and the other to Charles Addams. Maslin was one of many cartoonists—including Leo Cullum, Nick Downes, Sam Gross, Arnie Levin, Frank Modell, Peter Steiner, Mick Stevens, P. C. Vey, and Jack Ziegler—who first got into the magazine by selling concepts that made their way to Addams. When *New Yorker* cartoonist Ellis Rosen was criticized (more than once) on the grounds that he was no Charles Addams, he was tempted to respond, "Sometimes Charles Addams was no Charles Addams."

Maslin has no interest in being part of a collaborative process, but he acknowledges that it can work well for others.

> If Charles Addams, Helen Hokinson, and George Price had never existed, I might feel
> that cartoons created by a team are somehow less than. But those giants did exist and they
> did well with outside ideas, so I won't say their collaborations were better or worse than
> cartoons created by an individual cartoonist; they were just different. In general, though,
> I feel better about work I know has come from an individual. It's more meaningful (to
> me), more interesting.

Robert Leighton agrees. "The best *New Yorker* cartoonists," he said, "are writers who know how to draw and can create a body of work that says something about who they are." When I asked him about Charles Addams, he said, "Good question—I was shocked to learn that he worked with gag writers. But I suspect that the strength of his vision ensured that he got ideas or gags that were consistent with this vision." I pressed Leighton on the issue, asking what was wrong with creating a cartoon that's funny but doesn't reflect a specific outlook or personal perspective. Leighton said he could better explain his position with the following examples:

> Say there were two magazines that paid very well for their cartoons: one for gun owners and the other for golfers. A gag writer might send me some gun gags that were sure to sell, and I would absolutely turn those down—no way will I put my name to gags from a gun owner's point of view.[10] Another writer might send me golf gags: completely benign, and possibly very funny to the golf crowd. But I don't want to do those either. Not because I have anything against golf, but it's a subject about which I have nothing to say.

Mick Stevens resists collaborating because, he says, "It's always been a point of pride with me to do my own ideas." He has on rare occasions worked with a friend who had a funny idea, but only one such collaboration (with the writer Jenny Allen) led to a sale:

"We've changed our minds. We DO want to be a burden to you!"

Carolita Johnson is another *New Yorker* cartoonist who doesn't like drawing other people's ideas. "I can barely stand taking the time to bring my own ideas to life! I'd actually much rather have someone else draw my ideas. I draw because I have to." Johnson did, however, collaborate once with television and magazine writer Nell Scovell,[11] who provided the entire concept for this cartoon:

"*The New Yorker* published it," said Johnson, "but Nell declined the opportunity to receive any credit—she was just happy to see it in the magazine—so I'm glad I get to mention her now."

Like Mick Stevens, John Klossner takes pride in creating cartoons on his own. "Such pride may be foolish," he said, "but the cartoons I enjoy the most have a distinct 'voice' and individual style that you can't get by drawing up someone else's idea."

Christopher Weyant has been approached by many gag writers who want to collaborate, but he's not interested. "I don't want to be just the illustrator. I like creating something personal and confessional." Ellis Rosen also dislikes being "the hired hand" because "there's so little room for personal expression."

Drew Dernavich agrees. "When I think of my favorite cartoons," he says, "they're usually the work of an individual whose unique voice hasn't been diluted, or whose eccentric edges haven't been rounded off in the process of working with another person." Dernavich will collaborate on certain projects, but not on *New Yorker* cartoons:

> I like coming up with ideas—it's more enjoyable than drawing—so I'm not looking to outsource that part of the process. Once a stranger emailed me an idea and said he didn't want any credit or money for it. I drew it up and *The New Yorker* bought it, but I felt really uncomfortable about it once it was published, so I haven't done anything like that again.

When I asked Lars Kenseth if he thinks cartoons by someone who writes their own captions are inherently superior to those created by a team, he said, "Not at all. A team can be just as good if not better than a solo cartoonist. It's all about developing a voice, and if you can do that in a duo, great!" Nevertheless, he said, "the only person I've ever collaborated with is my wife, Liz, who came up with the idea behind this drawing, which *The New Yorker* published as a Daily Cartoon:"

He doesn't see that changing.

While I like being collaborative, and have fun with it on the regular as a TV writer, I'm a big believer in marinating in your own juices when it comes to cartoons. It helps you define your own comedic voice. Also, for me, cartooning is my creative life preserver. There's no executive to consult, no head writer to appease. I get to creatively rise or fall on my own. While I'll often look for feedback, or run a cartoon by someone to see if it's working, I always go with my gut because the caption I land on wasn't just a punch line I thought up in the car. It's built on years of thinking and drawing that I've done on my own.

Alex Gregory is, like Kenseth, a comedy writer, so I assumed he never collaborated with anyone on his cartoons. "Never is a strong word," he said. "I've had some writer friends pitch me ideas—I can think of four offhand that went straight into *The New Yorker* without my changing a word—and I've also submitted jokes to other artists. Shhhh."

Some *New Yorker* cartoonists enjoy collaborating on a regular basis, and such partnerships (which, for many years after 1973 were rare and something of a dirty secret) have become more common. Kaamran Hafeez works with, among others, Vin Coca, who co-hosts the caption contest podcast and provided the idea for this cartoon, which appeared in the magazine on September 5, 2022:

"I've always wanted to learn to swim, but it's never been more than thirty minutes since my last meal."

When I asked Hafeez what he likes about collaborating, he said,

It gives me time to do other things. When I started out, I wrote all my own material, but it took most of the day every day because I am not a prolific writer. I come to this profession from the drawing side. I've had to learn how to write jokes and it takes many hours or even days for me to come up with cartoons that are good enough to submit to *The New Yorker*. Collaborating with gag writers lets me enjoy a more balanced life. They do what they're good at, I do what I'm good at, and between the two of us we can create a terrific single-panel cartoon. I don't get to take all the credit, but then it's not about me—it's about a high-quality finished product that adds value to the magazine and to the readers' experience.

New Yorker cartoonist Sophie Lucido Johnson collaborates with Sammi Skol-moski, a staff writer at *The Onion*.

Sammi and I meet every other week, gossip for a while about our health problems and people we know, and then we go off to our own little corners and write for about an hour. We then return with a list of gag ideas—usually ten to twenty each. We read them to each other, and each of us gets to choose five that the other person wrote. Then we sit together and edit them, and later, I draw them.

When I asked what she likes about the collaborative process, she said,

I don't really believe that people are their best as individuals. I think we're better when we work together; it removes so much of the ego from the mix and leaves all of the fun. This process is never stressful, because Sammi and I crack each other up, and it's a joy to write together. Then, when our cartoons are rejected, we can be like, "They were wrong; that batch was gold." Much better than stewing about it alone.

The current cartoon editor welcomes such partnerships. In a Daily Shouts piece for aspiring *New Yorker* cartoonists, she wrote, "What if you're a master artist, but your buddy Philomena is the one with a real sense of humor. Can you team up? I don't see why not, so long as P-dawg is game and you make it clear that you collaborated."[12]

I wish that rule—"make it clear that you collaborated"—had existed earlier. After I won my fifth caption contest, a few *New Yorker* cartoonists reached out to me through Mankoff and we started working together, but I never got public credit for my contributions. Until now.

Gag Writer

I have collaborated with four *New Yorker* cartoonists: Harry Bliss, Peter Kuper, Felipe Galindo, and Lila Ash. I loved working with each of them and would have done it for free, but I kept that to myself and got paid for my captions and the occasional original concept.

HARRY BLISS

Bliss has been a staff cartoonist at *The New Yorker* since 1997. He also has a syndicated one-panel comic called *Bliss* that appears online and in newspapers every day, so he must constantly produce and it's no surprise he's open to working with gag writers. *The New Yorker* published four of our collaborations. Here are the first three:

"You call this guacamole?"

"Yes, I came back. I always come back."

"All parents fight."

I sent Bliss a few captions for that last cartoon, and he debated between the one he ultimately selected and *"Go see what your mother's screaming about."* He probably made the right choice—*The New Yorker* bought it—but I prefer, ever so slightly, the darker joke.

The New Yorker published our fourth and final collaboration on November 12, 2018:

"Good beard"... "Nice beard"... "Good beard"...
"Great beard"... "Good beard"...

Before explaining why that was our final collaboration, I want to highlight just five of the more than eighty cartoons (his drawings, my captions and, in a few cases, my concepts) that appeared in *Bliss*.

DRAWING: In the dungeon of a castle, where they have been banished, a court jester addresses the king's minstrel.
CAPTION: *"He likes music and he likes comedies, but he hates musical comedies."*

DRAWING: On a wooden raft in the middle of the ocean, an emaciated ship-wreck survivor is addressing his companion.
CAPTION: *"Well, if you don't want to discuss exposure, drowning, or sharks, what do you want to talk about?"*

DRAWING: A man is standing in the doorway of an office and addressing his boss, who's sitting at the desk with his head in his hands.
CAPTION: *"Sorry, I got that wrong. It's wife on Line 1, mistress on Line 2."*

DRAWING: Standing in the front doorway of his home, one demon is waving goodbye to another.
CAPTION: *"I'll see you in hell."*

DRAWING: At a graveside service, a priest is standing in front of the casket, holding a bible and addressing the bereaved.
CAPTION: *"The Lord giveth and the Lord taketh away. You just can't tell with the Lord."*

I suggested both the image and caption for those last two cartoons.

Bliss stopped working with me after he started collaborating exclusively with Steve Martin—yes, *that* Steve Martin. They subsequently published a collection of their work (*A Wealth of Pigeons*), and Bliss illustrated Martin's memoir, *Number One Is Walking*. Losing a job to Steve Martin—an accomplishment I've included on my résumé—is probably the most impressive thing I've done.

PETER KUPER

Kuper is a cartoonist, teacher, and the author of *Ruins*, which won the 2016 Eisner Award for best graphic novel. *The New Yorker* published three of our collaborations:

"It's an internship--crime doesn't pay."

"If she floats, she's a witch.
If she sinks, maybe she had a point about women's rights."

"Thank God for the elephant."

That last cartoon also appears in *The New Yorker Encyclopedia of Cartoons* under Q for "quicksand." When I asked Kuper what he likes about the collaborative process, he said,

> I enjoy taking credit for your ideas. Actually, I appreciate your ability to see my cartoon from a perspective I had never imagined. And when you're suggesting an original idea instead of providing a caption for one of my drawings, I like bringing your concepts to life. Working with you also reenergizes me when I'm running out of steam. Pitching cartoon ideas to *The New Yorker* every week while teaching and working on graphic novels is exhausting.

I hope Kuper and I will collaborate again. As far as I know, he hasn't yet tossed me aside for some famous comedian.

Felipe Galindo (Feggo)

The New Yorker bought but has not yet published one of our collaborations, so I can't reproduce it here. I can, however, show you one of our joint efforts that the magazine rejected:

"We can't stay here, and your father has connections in China."

It was subsequently published as the Last Laugh in an issue of *Reader's Digest*. I was happy for Feggo—a sale's a sale, and *Reader's Digest* has a global circulation of more than three million—but also embarrassed. In an episode of *Everybody Loves Raymond*, Ray's father sells a "humorous anecdote" to *Reader's Digest* and won't shut up about it.

The anecdote's awful, and the message running through the episode is that *Reader's Digest* is not funny.[1] But then our cartoon won second prize and $5,000 in the 2012 United Nations / Ranan Lurie Political Cartoon Awards contest. The judges included celebrated humorists Ban Ki-moon, eighth secretary general of the United Nations, and Elie Wiesel, author of *Night* and other hilarious reflections on the Holocaust.

LILA ASH

The New Yorker published one of our collaborations as the Daily Cartoon on February 7, 2020, when the country was grappling with the possibility that Donald Trump might win a second term in office:

"I feel bad for the national symbols that can't fly to Canada."

Our first collaboration, however, appeared in the magazine on December 16, 2019:

"We're SO not getting our security deposit back."

The next day, *The Daily Show* did a segment on prehistoric cave art that had recently been discovered in Sulawesi, Indonesia. About one minute into the segment, Trevor Noah said,

> What I really love about discovering ancient art in a cave is that it shows that cavemen were more creative than we think. It also shows that they didn't give a shit about their security deposit. Yeah, it's like screw it. We've got no heat, no water. I'm drawing on the walls.

People who saw both that episode of *The Daily Show* and Ash's cartoon got on Instagram to falsely accuse Noah (or his writers) of stealing our joke. That baseless accusation highlighted not the problem of joke theft, but the phenomenon of . . .

Parallel Thinking

Very few of the five thousand to ten thousand entries that *The New Yorker* receives for each week's contest are unique. Here's the winning caption from the contest that featured this drawing by Felipe Galindo:

"I will give you no quarter."
Timmy Booth, Seattle, Wash.

That's a good pun, but there were more than two hundred similar entries, including these three:

"I give no quarter."
"I give you no quarter."
"I will give you no quarters."

That last caption is especially clever because the coin box indicates that the ride costs fifty cents.

Different people often come up with the same joke at the same time. In the caption contest, my submission was identical to the winning entry three times:

"I'm working from home."

Mary Melton, Newton, Mass.

"Still not level."
Nathaniel Pierce, Trappe, Md.

"How soon can you start?"

John Maynard, Berkeley, Calif.

John Maynard, who received credit for that last caption, said the experience was so unpleasant he'll never enter the contest again: "Several people from around the country tracked me down through the phone book. One insisted that he came up with the caption first, and that it wasn't fair that I was getting the credit."[1] Let me state for the record that I was not the person who complained to Maynard. That person sounds like a lunatic.

Even Emma Allen, the current cartoon editor for *The New Yorker*, has been affected by parallel thinking. Her boyfriend entered the contest featuring this drawing by Michael Maslin:

His entry—"*Didn't you see the light?*"—was selected as one of the three finalists, but when Colin Stokes, who at the time was the associate cartoon editor, realized that Emma's boyfriend had submitted it, he feared charges of favoritism (even though the contest is judged blindly).[2] Fortunately, Martha Strauss, of Dunnerston, Vermont, had submitted the exact same caption, so she got credit and went on to win the popular vote.

The New Yorker works hard to ensure that it does not publish any cartoon that is identical or even similar to one that has already appeared in the magazine. On January 20, 2014, however, the magazine published this cartoon by Tom Toro:

"Why isn't my car horn magically fixing everything?"

Look familiar? It did to one of my friends, who called to say that Toro stole my *"Try honking again"* joke, which had appeared in the magazine about three years earlier. She was wrong. Both Toro and I were commenting on the same futile behavior, but he independently came up with a joke that mocks people who think honking is an effective way to get traffic moving.

Because *New Yorker* cartoonists have to come up with so many concepts every week, they run the risk of making a joke that's been made before or even, without meaning to, recycling their own material. When I was collaborating with Harry Bliss, he asked me to caption his drawing of a factory owner addressing his young son as they look out over huge industrial smokestacks. I suggested, *"Someday, son, all this will be your fault."* He used that caption for the cartoon that appeared in *Bliss* on November 5, 2016, and less than a year later it reappeared in *Bliss* with a younger, taller, more casually-dressed father. I emailed Bliss to let him know, and he wrote back, "Shit!" He had forgotten all about the first cartoon.

When you submit an entry to the caption contest, you're almost certainly one of many people who are making the same joke. To get selected as a finalist, therefore, you have to deliver the joke really well. Even then, of course, you may not make it to the finalists' round, which can make you feel like . . .

You Got Robbed

If you're surprised or frustrated or angered every week *The New Yorker* overlooks your caption, you're not alone. The magazine's editors are regularly excoriated, privately and publicly, for choosing the wrong captions and ignoring superior entries. On June 25, 2019, Emmy-winning screenwriter Ken Levine (*Cheers*, *Frasier*, *The Simpsons*) took to his blog to vent about his experience with the contest:

> A very prominent comedy writer and I used to submit. We would run our captions by each other to make sure they were good enough [and] send them in. And then nothing. Neither of us was ever a finalist. Did I think my entries were better than those selected? Most of the time. Sometimes I thought the ones they picked were terrific. . . . But like I said, we never broke through. So what did we do? Instead of getting mad, and challenging their selection process, we simply stopped submitting.

Levine then started drawing his own cartoons and, in 2022, *The New Yorker* started publishing them:

"He who controls the Internet controls the world."

"I may look goofy, but I'm in the New York Times crossword
puzzle way more than Alan Alda."

If you can't draw, however, the contest remains your best chance of making it into the magazine, and you have to get used to rejection and sometimes seeing an inferior caption get selected as a finalist. It's unfair but inevitable. *The New Yorker* has less than a week to review five thousand to ten thousand captions, many of which may get overlooked because they don't do well enough in crowdsourcing to catch the editors' attention. Even captions that come in first during crowdsourcing get passed over. Here was my entry for the contest that featured this cartoon by Felipe Galindo:

"I don't care what Satan lets his kids do."

It was the top-rated caption in crowdsourcing but failed to make the finalists' round. I shouldn't complain because I've managed over the years to do relatively well, but I've also lost more than eight hundred contests and each time I've been indignant (usually without cause).

Sometimes you make it to the finalists' round with a perfectly-worded caption that not only reconciles the disparate frames of reference but is actually funny, and then lose to a caption that's good—maybe very good—but not as deserving as yours. Contest No. 815 featured this drawing by Farley Katz:

Paul Nesja, who co-hosts the caption contest podcast, became a finalist by suggesting that the smiling whale had initially proposed an impractical alternative to a beach vacation: *"And you wanted to go to the mountains."* A majority of the voters, however, preferred this climate catastrophe joke by Dustin Charles, of Washington, D.C.: *"A few more years, and all this will be ours."* I like that winning caption, but I love Paul's runner-up.

Hundreds of worthy captions don't even make it to the finalists' round, and it's time to give at least some of them the recognition they deserve:

"It was a phone interview."

"You're it."

"*The kids seem quiet.*"

"Your stomach is still growling."

That last caption, by Beth Lawler, is extremely close to the winning entry: *"Your stomach is growling."* Usually I prefer shorter captions, but in this case the slightly longer version is superior because the word "still" suggests that the snake's stomach was growling both before and after he ate, but for entirely different reasons. You, of course, may disagree because . . .

Humor Is Subjective

People who vote during the crowdsourcing stage of the caption contest never reach anything close to consensus, even when it comes to highly-rated submissions. Here is the winning entry from a contest that featured this drawing by Lars Kenseth:

"Looks like an inside, inside, inside, inside, inside job."
Ryan Spiers, San Francisco, Calif.

Though it was among the top 1.5 percent of entries in crowdsourcing, it received a shockingly low percentage of "Funny" votes:

FUNNY	SOMEWHAT FUNNY	NOT FUNNY
13%	29%	58%

These results confirm that many people will dislike a joke that others find funny, but they don't explain why. Here are my theories, at least in the context of crowdsourcing:

Some people aren't funny. Prior to crowdsourcing, the contest entries were evaluated by people Mankoff described as "crack humor specialists."[1] That's no longer the case. The specialists don't get involved until after the first stage of judging the contest is complete, and anyone can participate in the initial stage. Unfortunately, many participants are not funny and, worse, can't recognize what is.

Some people are unduly harsh. Constant judging can make you excessively and sometimes thoughtlessly critical. When you're voting on captions during the crowdsourcing stage of the contest, you're making snap judgments. You're not taking time to appreciate the entries, and if you come across one that's terrific but takes awhile to sink in, you'll likely dismiss it as "Not Funny." You may also dismiss entries that are variations on, or even superior versions of, captions you've already rated "Funny" because the joke no longer seems fresh.

Some people are underhanded bastards. Some people who vote during crowd-sourcing have entered the contest and may be trying to increase their chances of winning by knocking out the competition. They may therefore dismiss as "Not Funny" an entry that's similar to theirs or is different but really good.

Another explanation—one that's not specific to the contest—is that no joke goes over well with everyone. Mankoff highlighted this fact at a TED Talk with the help of a *New Yorker* cartoon by David Sipress:[2]

That seems like a cartoon everyone would appreciate, but one man disliked it so much he wrote an angry letter: "Another joke on old white males. Ha ha. The wit. It's nice, I'm sure to be young and rude, but someday you'll be old, unless you drop dead as I wish." When Mankoff displayed that comment on the screen, everyone in the audience laughed—in part, Mankoff suggested, because they were part of a group and the laughter was contagious. But the dynamic changes when a person is alone.

Mankoff is used to negative feedback. Many of the letters he received as cartoon editor were complaints from readers who found a joke offensive. The rest were complaints from readers who didn't understand the cartoon or find it funny.[3] There was apparently no fan mail.

Some of the most easily-offended people are animal lovers. Mankoff conducted an online survey to gauge the public's response to this cartoon by Mike Twohy:

"Discouraging data on the antidepressant."

Most people (about 85 percent) thought it was funny. But others found it objectionable, including the person who wrote, "I like animals!!!!! I don't want to hurt them. . . . That doesn't seem very funny to me." Someone else wrote, "I don't like to see animals suffer—even in cartoons."

Paul Nesja, who co-hosts the caption contest podcast, criticized the following caption, which made it to the finalists' round, as insensitive to people who have struggled with addiction:[4]

"He's going to need more drugs."
Brandon Lawniczak, Mill Valley, Calif.

Paul's not humorless, but his criticism was unfair. Lawniczak's caption did not make light of a serious problem. It simply reconciled the disparate frames of reference: operating rooms (where drugs are used to anesthetize patients) and '70s-era discos (where cocaine was the drug of choice). Many cartoons touch on grim subjects—war, death, murder, suicide, alcoholism, addiction, divorce, mental illness—without being mean-spirited. Contest No. 12 featured this drawing by Mick Stevens, one of many "man on the ledge" cartoons that have appeared in the magazine:

Is that insensitive to people who have lost a loved one to suicide? Of course not—no more than a cartoon about divorce is insensitive to children whose parents split up.[5]

There are, however, limits. After 9/11, *The New Yorker* got some very funny anti-terrorist jokes, and the best came from Sam Gross. It's set in heaven, where the prophet Muhammad is addressing a suicide bomber who's been blown to pieces: *"You'll get the virgins when we find your penis."* Mankoff loved that cartoon but couldn't publish it because, he said, "*The New Yorker* is a serious magazine. If you've just read fifty thousand words by Seymour Hirsch on terrorism, that joke would seem inappropriate."[6] But remember my friend Chris, who mocked me for misinterpreting the "Grim Reaper with a plate of lemons" cartoon? In Contest No. 191, he made it to the finalists' round with this reference to the heavenly reward for jihadist martyrs:

"Just to confirm—I get seventy-two lemmings, right?"
Chris Norborg, Chicago, Ill.

Anti-Humor

Anti-humor is not the opposite of humor or a movement opposed to anything funny, as exemplified by the angry woman in the John Callahan cartoon who yells, "This is a feminist bookstore. There *is* no humor section!"[1] It's a type of comedy that subverts the expectations established by traditional humor, and it's been used for years to parody the caption contest.

In 2007, journalist and author Daniel Radosh, who had been contributing to *The New Yorker* for ten years, created *The Anti-Caption Contest*, which solicited the worst possible captions for each week's cartoon. Here's just one example, featuring a drawing by Mick Stevens:

"It's too expensive to dump boiling oil on rioters these days,
so we had to switch to these counterfeit bills covered in poison.
This actually works better because they don't drop dead
until they're back home, so we don't even have to clean up the bodies."

Another example of contest-related anti-humor is *The Monkeys You Ordered*,[2] a website that features literal descriptions of what's happening in the cartoons:

*"Your car won't start because there are a bunch of
clowns and one non-clown guy inside the hood."*

The Monkeys You Ordered is funny, but it's a one-note joke.

Another one-note joke is the universal caption. In 2006, Charles Lavoie convincingly argued that *"Christ, what an asshole"* could be used to caption every drawing that appears in the contest. It certainly works for this Tom Chitty cartoon:

"Christ, what an asshole."

Lavoie was the first but not the only person to propose a universal caption. Cory Arcangel, a digital artist who was once the subject of a *New Yorker* profile,[3] suggested, *"What a misunderstanding!"*[4] Frank Chimero proposed, *"Hi. I'd like to add you to my professional network on LinkedIn,"*[5] and less than two weeks later it appeared in *The New Yorker* as the caption for this cartoon by Liam Francis Walsh:

"Hi, I'd like to add you to my professional network on LinkedIn."

Walsh's original caption was, "*Farmer Brown? It's your wake-up call.*" That line makes a lot more sense than Frank Chimero's universal caption, but it fell victim to a prank. During one of Mankoff's weekly meetings with David Remnick, who had the final say on all cartoons, Mankoff replaced the captions for the first ten drawings with Chimero's LinkedIn joke, and Remnick said "What the fuck is this?" Mankoff explained, and Remnick said, "Let's use one."[6]

Even some *New Yorker* cartoonists have come up with universal captions: Matt Diffee ("*You may not remember me, but we went to high school together.*"); Emily Flake ("*My body being riddled with tumors, this seems insignificant.*"); Zachary Kanin ("*Surprise!*" or "*Surprise.*" or "*Surprise?*"); Kim Warp ("*I don't get this cartoon, but I'm in it.*"); and Farley Katz ("*Who farted?*").[7] Emily Flake's sick joke works best, and I've used it here to caption Christopher Weyant's cartoon from Contest No. 789:

"*My body being riddled with tumors, this seems insignificant.*"

The most popular example of anti-humor, at least in the context of the caption contest, is *Shitty New Yorker Cartoon Captions*, which has more than 94,000 followers on Instagram. It's the brainchild of Willy Staley and Matt Jordan, both of whom started entering the contest in earnest more than ten years ago but, after failing to make it to the finalists' round, changed course. Their goal is no longer to win the contest, but to submit the most vulgar and hilariously inappropriate captions possible. Here is just one example of their work:

"Says here I gotta cut your nuts off."

Unlike other parodies, *Shitty New Yorker Cartoon Captions* is not a one-note joke. Staley and Jordan work hard to come up with entries that will never win the contest but are funnier than many that do. It's also not, as some people assume, the creation of two people who hate the caption contest. "I would love to win," said Jordan.

> I see a lot of comments online that suggest our followers think we're performing a deep critique of *The New Yorker* or its cartoons. I don't see *Shitty New Yorker Cartoon Captions* like that at all. What it is to me is a fun writing project with my friend that we get a kick out of. What it's not is a mean-spirited critique of *The New Yorker* or its cartoonists. . . . although, maybe it *is* a critique of the winning captions."[8]

Speaking of such critiques, let's take a look at puns.

Puns

In 2004, when the caption contest was still an annual event, Alex Gregory's drawing of a giant squid at a sushi bar elicited more than thirteen thousand entries. *The New Yorker* noted that many were puns, "which, like most puns, ranged from the execrable to the slightly less execrable."[1] The magazine then turned the contest into a weekly competition, and for the next decade puns fared poorly. *The New Yorker* didn't select one as a finalist until Contest No. 20, which featured this drawing by Mick Stevens:

"We met at the minibar."

Paul Cretien, Waco, Texas

The next appeared in Contest No. 40, which featured a Harry Bliss cartoon:

"Well, that was abominable."

Carl Gable, Norcross, Ga.

That trend continued for years, with puns making it to the finalists' round only about 5 percent of the time, indicating that most are clever rather than funny. Even John Pollock, a former presidential speechwriter for Bill Clinton and author of *The*

Pun Also Rises—How the Humble Pun Revolutionized Language, Changed History, and Made Wordplay More Than Some Antics, concedes that puns are "often more about getting an 'Aha!' than a 'Haha!'"[2] "The trouble with puns," wrote P. J. O'Rourke, who served as editor in chief at *National Lampoon* and reviewed Pollock's book for *The New York Times*, "is they're cute. Humor has nothing to do with cute."[3]

Why, then, did puns suddenly start doing so well in the caption contest? The answer is crowdsourcing. As noted previously, voters who participate in this process typically move quickly, making split-second decisions about which captions are very or mildly or not at all funny. Under those conditions, puns tend to do well because voters get them immediately. Captions that receive "Funny" votes appear more frequently—a function of the crowdsourcing algorithm—while captions that require a little thought get dismissed as "Not Funny" and disappear before other voters get a chance to see them, recognize how good they are, and rate them accordingly.

Here is a small but representative sample of puns that won the contest soon after *The New Yorker* started using crowdsourcing:

"*Your overhead is going to kill you.*"
Carolyn Beck, Toronto, Ont.

"I admire your restraint."
Linda Pickering, Lawrenceville, N.J.

"Long time, no sea."
Carlos Brooks, Los Angeles, Calif.

The pun's repeated success in the contest had a pronounced effect, encouraging people to submit short and easily understood captions that are designed to do well in crowdsourcing instead of more creative jokes that take a moment to sink in. Nicole Chrolavicius, who has been a finalist ten times since she started competing in 2020, describes this phenomenon from a personal perspective:

> When I first started entering the contest, I read articles and watched videos by and about people who won. Most advised against entering puns. I followed this advice and wrote what I considered to be my funniest captions, but they were never chosen as finalists. I was also studying the captions that made it to the finalists' rounds, and I saw that nearly every week a pun was selected. I therefore changed course and started submitting puns.

Her strategy worked, and she won the contest featuring this cartoon by Paul Noth:

"They call it kitsch and release."
Nicole Chrolavicius, Burlington, Ont.

Puns have their place but, like exclamation points, they should be used sparingly. My critical attitude toward them comes, in part, from my experience in Contest No. 742, which featured this drawing by Tim Hamilton:

After making it to the finalists' round with "*Fine, but no flash photography*," I lost to a triple pun from Benjamin Branfman, of New York City: "*That's a rare medium. Well done.*" Voters impressed by Branfman's wordplay overlooked the discrepancy between his caption, which has the security guard offering congratulations, and the guard's expression, which suggests he's issuing a warning.

Though I'm generally averse to puns, I love this one:

"It's a thongbird."
Sandy Sommer, St. Louis, Mo.

So did *The New Yorker*'s editors. Not only did they select it as a finalist in Contest No. 103; they declared it the best contest-winning caption of 2007.[4]

Rise of the Machines

The Cartoon Caption Contest has generated an enormous amount of data—readers have submitted a total of more than five million captions to hundreds of contests—and scientists are mining that data for experiments designed to determine whether an artificial intelligence program can develop a sense of humor. Jerry Seinfeld, who doesn't think it's possible to teach people—let alone computers—how to be funny, would almost certainly say it cannot.

Dafna Shahaf would disagree. She is an associate professor of computer science at The Hebrew University of Jerusalem. In her work, she uses massive amounts of data to help computers emulate the human capacity to understand humor. In 2014, when she was a senior researcher at Microsoft, she attended a lecture by Mankoff about the caption contest archive and wondered whether it could be used to teach a computer to accurately assess whether a given caption is funny. She was trying to solve one of the most challenging problems in machine learning—how to teach a computer to recognize sarcasm, wordplay, and other forms of humor and thereby communicate more effectively.

A computer's inability to understand jokes can have real consequences. On April 1, 2015, Tesla tweeted, as an April Fools' Day joke, that it was creating a rival to the Apple Watch called the Model W, a new device that not only tells the time and date but is adjustable—in other words, a watch. Because algorithmic trading systems cannot detect humor, let alone sarcasm, the tweet led to a surge in Tesla stock prices.[1]

Shahaf teamed up with Mankoff and another Microsoft researcher, Eric Horvitz, to conduct a study using thousands of drawings and captions from *The New Yorker* database. The results were published in a paper called "Inside Jokes: Identifying Humorous Cartoon Captions." The researchers were able to develop a software system that could winnow out many of the worst entries, approximately 45 percent of the total, which means *The New Yorker*'s cartoon department could use it to eliminate at least 2,200 submissions every week.

"Inside Jokes" was not the only research paper Mankoff helped write. In 2016 he teamed up with professors from the University of Michigan and Columbia University and researchers from Yahoo! Labs to take a "computational approach" to understanding humor and learn what differentiates funny captions from the rest. The results of their study—set forth in a paper titled, "Humor in Collective Discourse: Unsupervised Funniness Detection in the New Yorker Cartoon Caption Contest"—will, the authors hope, help scientists design "more engaging conversational agents in text and multimodal (vision+text) systems." I'm not sure what that means, but it sounds like a positive development.

More recently, AI experts and members of the Peabody Award–winning digital publisher The Pudding tried to determine whether a computer could produce better-than-average cartoon captions. Using GPT-3, a computer language model that employs "deep-learning," which imitates the way human beings gain certain types of knowledge, to produce humanlike text, they tried to create or help humans create a winning caption. GPT-3 has a text box that generates responses to any written prompt.

My sister tested the program by entering the prompt, "Lawrence Wood New Yorker Caption Contest." The response was humbling:

> I'm sorry, I'm not aware of a person named Lawrence Wood who has been involved with the caption contest feature in The New Yorker magazine. . . . The [weekly] cartoon caption contest has been running in the magazine since 2005, and many different people have submitted captions over the years. It's possible that Lawrence Wood may have submitted a caption to the contest, but without more information, I cannot confirm this.

To generate a caption for this drawing by Drew Dernavich,

the team entered the following text:

WRITE A FUNNY CAPTION FOR A NEW YORKER CARTOON.
CARTOON DESCRIPTION: A COUPLE ARE SITTING ON A COUCH AND EACH ONE IS HOLD-
ING A REMOTE. THEY'RE SURROUNDED BY FIVE GUYS WHO ARE SWEEPING THE FLOOR
AROUND THE COUCH LOOKING FOR METAL. THE WOMAN IS SAYING SOMETHING TO THE
MAN.

GPT-3 responded with, *"I'm telling you, I don't know how the remote controls keep getting lost."* Not great, but not terrible for a machine. It's essentially a longer and clunkier version of *"Honey, the remote is in your hand,"* which *The New Yorker* selected as a finalist. (It was submitted by Tony Pechi, of San Diego, California.) By refining the prompt the team got better responses, including:

> *"If I didn't know better I'd think you were hiding something."*
> *"Anything? No? Then let's see who's buried in the back."*
> *"I don't think we should use our silverware tonight."*

They're not as good as the winning caption from Aaron Sherman, of St. Louis, Missouri (*"Don't worry about it—I wasn't going to say yes anyway."*) but they're not bad.

The team then submitted computer-generated captions to ten actual *New Yorker* contests to see how they would fare in crowdsourcing. (The Pudding was conducting an experiment so it gets a pass, but submitting captions that have been created with the assistance of a computer program violates both the spirit and letter of the contest rules, which provide that, "Entrants represent and warrant that their Submission is their original work.") Only one caption did somewhat well, placing among the top two hundred entries in a contest that elicited more than seven thousand submissions. The Pudding published the results of its study in an article titled, "We Couldn't Get an Artificial Intelligence Program to Win the New Yorker Caption Contest."

The most recent scientific study to rely on data from the caption contest confirmed that AI programs still lag far behind humans when it comes to humor. Researchers challenged AI models and humans to complete tasks such as matching cartoons to their winning captions and explaining why those captions were funny. The humans crushed the competition.

The results of the study (to which Mankoff contributed) appear in "Do Androids Laugh at Electric Sheep? Humor 'Understanding' Benchmarks from the New Yorker Cartoon Caption Contest," which won a best-paper award at the sixty-first annual meeting of the Association for Computational Linguistics. Computer scientist Yejin Choi, a 2022 recipient of the MacArthur "genius" grant, co-authored the paper and concluded that "even the fanciest A.I. today cannot really decipher what's going on in *New Yorker* captions."[2] I find that reassuring, but the day when a computer program can understand humor, and even win the caption contest, may not be that far off.

Afterword

A few months after *The New Yorker Radio Hour* debuted on October 24, 2015, host David Remnick introduced a short segment by saying,

> Here's a guy I want to meet, and I want you to meet. His name is Larry Wood and he is a master, the all-time greatest, the champ at something very specific: *The New Yorker* Caption Contest. . . . He is the Muhammad Ali and the Joe Louis and the Ronda Rousey of the contest. There's no one even close. How does he do it?[1]

I hope this book provided a satisfying answer while also showing what can be learned from the contest. The most obvious lesson is that thousands of people want to see their names in the magazine and become a permanent part of a *New Yorker* cartoon. I understand that desire. When I wrote an article on how to win the contest for a special cartoon issue of *The New Yorker*, Roz Chast drew a picture of me for the contributors' page[2]:

CONTRIBUTORS

NEIMA JAHROMI

is a fact-checker at *The New Yorker* by day and writes by night. He also flies by night, has it on your desk by morning, and drinks coffee by mid-afternoon.

JULIA WERTZ

is a professional cartoonist, a part-time urban explorer, and an amateur historian. She lives in Greenpoint, Brooklyn.

LAWRENCE WOOD

is a civil legal-aid attorney. He also teaches a poverty-law seminar at the University of Chicago, which Justice Antonin Scalia dismissed as a waste of time.

ROZ CHAST

is a cartoonist for *The New Yorker* and has written several books. Likes: birds, origami, art, things that are funny, New York, grilled cheese, the ocean. Dislikes: coconut, writing bios.

EDWARD STEED

has been drawing cartoons for *The New Yorker* for more than two years. He wears gray on the outside 'cause gray is how he feels on the inside.

LIANA FINCK

wears pinck, draws in inck, and takes her showers in the sinck. Her graphic novel, "A Bintel Brief" (Ecco Press), was published in 2014.

EMILY FLAKE

was a summer-school gym-class girls' badminton champion in 1994. She is also a cartoonist for *The New Yorker*, and has recently published a book about parenting called "Mama Tried" (Grand Central Publishing).

I framed that picture and hung it in my house where every visitor can notice it without my having to say, "Hey, did you see this?"[3]

There are, of course, more important lessons. Lars Kenseth derives hope from the thousands of people who want to participate in the creation of something funny. "Whenever I post a caption contest cartoon on Instagram my comments section explodes with entries. I get more engagement out of those cartoons than any others I post. People want to join in the fun, and that's such a heartening thing. It makes me think that maybe we're not so terrible after all." P. C. Vey agrees. "Everyone seems to love the contest, and people ask me about it all the time. In this day and age, when there are so many reasons to despair, I find their joy and enthusiasm inspiring."

Robert Leighton draws inspiration from the fact that there are so many solutions to a challenging puzzle. "It helps me understand that, when I don't have a good idea for one of my own cartoons, I should keep the drawing 'open' and let it percolate. Something is out there, maybe something perfect." For Christopher Weyant, the contest shows that "most people have a deep desire to create and make others laugh. Granted, some folks are funnier than others or more inventive about it, but the contest is a joyous experiment in something uniquely human—the joke. I'm sure we were trying to add the perfect line to cave paintings forty thousand years ago." Mick Stevens, whose cartoon appears on the cover of this book, had the same thought:

Back in 2005, Ben Greenman, an editor at *The New Yorker*, asked Mankoff whether the weekly caption contest might serve as "a kind of ongoing laboratory" to "get a better sense of how the human comic mind works." "I hope so," said Mankoff.

> If there's anything in any way funny about a drawing—it may not rise to the level of a great cartoon, but it's there—thousands of people looking at it will find that angle and attempt to explain it in some way. Plus, if we do it for seventy-five years, we can track how humor changes over time.[4]

The contest hasn't been around that long, but it is already serving as a kind of ongoing laboratory. Scientists and academics are using data generated by hundreds of contests and millions of entries to help determine not only "how the human comic mind works," but whether a computer program can learn to be funny, or at least recognize humor, and therefore improve its ability to communicate.

I don't know from computers, but I know about single-panel cartoons, and for the past twenty-five years *The New Yorker*'s caption contest has produced many that are terrific. More than 150 of the best appear in this book, but a lot of equally fine ones are missing. I looked at the winning cartoons from the first 864 weekly contests and found 282 (almost a third) that are, in my opinion, good enough to appear as regular cartoons in the magazine. Including them all here, however, would have made this book far too long.

The challenge presented by each contest can seem insurmountable, especially when the drawing presents a scenario that is, like this one by Joe Dator, simply baffling:[5]

Barry Hodges, of Cashmere, Washington, focused on a minor detail in the cartoon and submitted one of my favorite contest-winning captions: *"Elbows on the table. Another reason I don't like broccoli."* That's almost as good as E. B. White's broccoli joke.

"If you have a talent for the contest," says Mankoff, "your brain starts to itch when you see a captionless drawing." I know that feeling. I get it every Monday morning when a new contest appears online. I send my ideas to brutally honest friends (their negative feedback includes comments like, "My God, that's awful," "You should be ashamed," and "I wish we'd never met"), submit an entry I'm sure will win, realize during crowdsourcing that my joke isn't as good as some of the competition, and wait, usually in vain, for an email from *The New Yorker* stating, "Congratulations! Your caption has been selected as one of the three finalists in this week's caption contest." When I don't get that email, I look at the entries that were selected and usually have to concede that at least one of them is better than what I submitted. Every week, however, presents a new challenge and another chance to become a finalist, and I always take advantage of that opportunity.

I hope you'll join me.

Acknowledgments

My wife convinced me not to call this book *The Finalist's Solution*. Every Monday morning I send to her and seven of my friends—Alan Alop, Jessica Kalmewicki, Chris Norborg, Jennifer Payne, Alice Setrini, Eli Wade-Scott, and Rachel Wilf-Townsend—three or more captions for the week's contest and ask them to help me select the best one. I appreciate their advice, honesty, and patience.

After reading an early draft of my manuscript, my friend Miriam Hallbauer said "This seems like a real book" and gave me permission to use that comment as a blurb. Another friend, Jon Tabor, contributed nothing to this book but begged to be mentioned in the acknowledgments.

Eric Rayman, a lawyer whose practice focuses on media and publishing (and who was formerly *The New Yorker*'s general counsel), read an early draft of this book. He liked it enough to schedule a meeting with me, Bob Mankoff, and Daniel Greenberg, a literary agent who represents *The Onion* and some of the funniest people alive, including Patton Oswalt, Demetri Martin, and Simon Rich. I don't know why Daniel wanted to also represent me, but I'm glad he did.

Hannah Phillips, my editor at St. Martin's Press, almost spit coffee on her keyboard while reading what my father yelled at me after I came home drunk during my senior year of high school. She also made this book much better than the manuscript she initially reviewed.

Thanks to all the cartoonists, contest judges, and contest-winners who took time to answer my questions. I'm especially grateful to Michael Maslin, whose *Ink Spill* website (michaelmaslin.com) is an incredible trove of information about *New Yorker* cartoons and cartoonists.

I am forever indebted to the artists whose cartoons got me into *The New Yorker*, either through the contest or as a result of our actual collaborations. Felipe Galindo, Peter Kuper, and Lila Ash gave me the originals of our joint efforts, and I can't thank them enough. Many thanks also to Harry Bliss for the lewd drawings he included in our correspondence. I'd frame and hang them on the walls of my house if they weren't so inappropriate.

CartoonStock's first marketing director, Jessica Ziegler (the daughter of *New Yorker* legend Jack Ziegler), supported Mankoff's decision to pay me to write caption contest commentaries for the company's website. When she left CartoonStock, *New Yorker* cartoonist Trevor Hoey assumed her position and the task of communicating with me on a regular basis. Working with Jessica and Trevor was and is a pleasure.

Bob, thanks for absolutely everything.

I wish my parents, who loved *New Yorker* cartoons, could see this book. I'm glad my sister and her family will get to read it, but they shouldn't expect free copies.

Notes

Introduction

1. "The Sunday Call Will Pay $20 for the Best Title for This Picture," *The San Francisco Call*, January 7, 1912.

2. "$1000.00 in Prizes," *New-York Tribune*, November 7, 1920.

3. Ramin Setoodeh, "Behind the Scenes: At the Caption Contest," *Newsweek*, December 10, 2006.

4. Russell Adams, "How About Never—Is Never Good for You? Celebrities Struggle to Write Winning Captions," *The Wall Street Journal*, September 10, 2011.

5. Roger Ebert, "I Finally Won the *New Yorker* Cartoon Caption Competition," *The Guardian*, May 1, 2011.

6. On February 3, 2003, more than four years before I won my first caption contest, *The New Yorker* published a letter I wrote in response to Scott Turow's article on capital punishment:

   Scott Turow's case against capital punishment is all the more convincing because he realizes that the desire to execute a killer is not "the product of an alien morality" but an impulse that he can recognize in himself ("To Kill or Not to Kill," January 6th). As Turow argues, however, the death penalty has never been, and can never be, imposed fairly, and its existence virtually guarantees that some innocent person will eventually be executed. Like Turow (who lives in Illinois, where the outgoing governor recently commuted all current death sentences to life imprisonment after several death row inmates were exonerated), many people can picture themselves in the role of executioner when it comes to ending the life of a wanton murderer. But they recoil at the thought of supporting a system under which a person can be killed for a crime he did not commit.
   Lawrence D. Wood
   Chicago, Ill.

7. *The Daily Show with Jon Stewart*, April 8, 2010.

8. Peter Schjeldahl, "Bare Naked Ladies," *The New Yorker*, October 17, 2011.

9. Jen Carlson, "*New Yorker* Caption Contest with Jonathan Ames," *Gothamist*, Sep 27, 2011.

10. "How to Write a New Yorker Cartoon Caption: Child-Prodigy Edition," *How to Write a New Yorker Cartoon Caption*, season 1, episode 5, April 26, 2018.

11. Megan McCluskey, "The Internet Can't Stop Laughing at This 9-Year-Old Girl's Cartoon Captions," *Time*, April 5, 2018, https://time.com/5229237/new-yorker-caption-contest-9-year-old-girl/.

12. Adam Gopnik, "Scenes from the Life of Roz Chast," *The New Yorker*, December 30, 2019.

13. "And the Winner Is," *The New Yorker*, February 7, 2000.

14. "The Cartoon Caption Contest," *The New Yorker*, November 22, 1999.

15. Steve Johnson, "Chicagoan Vies for 3rd *New Yorker* Win," *Chicago Tribune*, June 1, 2009; Steve Johnson, "Chicagoan Scores a Triple Play in *New Yorker* Contest," *Chicago Tribune*, June 2, 2009.

16. Alex Altman, "How to Win the *New Yorker* Caption Contest," *Time*, June 8, 2009.

17. Roger Ebert, "The New Yorker. No, The New Yorker," www.rogerebert.com, July 16, 2009.

18. "Nobody Writes a Caption Like Larry Wood," *The New Yorker Radio Hour*, January 15, 2016.

19. Mankoff invited me to New York City for the website's launch party, so I flew in and took a taxi from the airport to the event. Stepping out of the cab I miscalculated the distance to the street, tripped, and fell down. Later that evening, a reporter who was covering the event approached me and asked, "Hey, aren't you the guy who fell out of the cab?" "Yes," I admitted. "I'd hoped no one saw." "I saw," he said, "and I've been telling *everybody*."

How It All Began

1. "Your Caption Here," *The New Yorker*, April 24, 2005.

2. Futterman immediately capitalized on his success by creating a list of captions (including "You are doing something unusual, Harold!") that would likely win future contests. Roy Futterman, "Future Winners of the *New Yorker* Cartoon Caption Contest," *McSweeney's Internet Tendency*, June 24, 2005.

Choosing the Drawings

1. "Your Caption Here," *The New Yorker*, April 24, 2005.

Choosing the Finalists

1. Robinson was part of a Chicago sketch-comedy group that, in 2010, made a pilot for Comedy Central called *My Mans*. They filmed the first scene at my agency's downtown office because the director was married to my colleague

Jenna. After watching the pilot, a network executive described our office as the ideal "nondescript, dead-end, and uninspired" setting for a show about disgruntled employees.

2. RJ Casey, "Checking In with Zach Kanin," *The Comics Journal*, January 22, 2018.

3. Ramin Setoodeh, "Behind the scenes: At the Caption Contest," *Newsweek*, December 10, 2006.

4. Adam Moerder, "What is a Hero?" *The New Yorker*, October 18, 2009.

5. Robert Mankoff, "The Caption Contest Sing-Along," Cartoon Desk, *The New Yorker*, February 20, 2013.

6. "Win the Caption Contest," *The New Yorker*, newyorker.com/video/watch/win-the-caption-contest.

7. Russell Adams, "How About Never—Is Never Good for You? Celebrities Struggle to Write Winning Captions," *The Wall Street Journal*, September 10, 2011.

CROWDSOURCING

1. "How Lazy Am I?," *The Cartoon Lounge*, season 4, episode 11.

2. "Help!," *The Cartoon Lounge*, season 4, episode 6.

IS THERE A PRIZE?

1. Roger Ebert, "Ebert's Moment of Glory: He Finally Wins Caption Contest," *Chicago Sun-Times*, April 27, 2011.

2. "Help! We Need You to Choose the Funniest Cartoon Contest Entries," Cartoon Desk, *The New Yorker*, March 23, 2016.

3. "Help!," *The New Yorker's Cartoon Lounge*, season 4, episode 6.

4. "In 1999, for five hundred points, a pair of physics students built a working nuclear breeder reactor in a Burton-Judson dorm room in one day, converting thorium powder collected from the inside of vacuum tubes into weapons-grade uranium, using a device made from scrap aluminum and carbon sheets. A concerned nuclear physicist attested to the machine's efficacy." Patricia Marx, "The Hunger Games," *The New Yorker*, June 25, 2012.

VARIATIONS ON A THEME

1. Robert Mankoff, "No Cliché is an Island," Cartoon Desk, *The New Yorker*, August 30, 2013.

2. Robert Mankoff, "No Cliché is an Island: The Thrilling Conclusion," Cartoon Desk, *The New Yorker*, September 13, 2013.

3. Robert Mankoff, "Long Story Long," Cartoon Desk, *The New Yorker*, September 20, 2013.

4. Robert Mankoff, "You'll Always Have Paris (If You Enter This Contest)," Cartoon Desk, *The New Yorker*, September 27, 2013.

5. Robert Mankoff, "We'll Always Have Reverse-Caption Contests," Cartoon Desk, *The New Yorker*, October 4, 2013.

6. Bob Eckstein and Michael Shaw, "The Cartoon Pad w/ guest Sam Gross," June 28, 2021, in *The Cartoon Pad* podcast, https://weeklyhumorist.com/the-cartoon-pad-w-guest-sam-gross/.

7. Daniel E. Slotnick, "Sam Gross, 89, Dies; Prolific Purveyor of Cartoons, Tasteful and Otherwise," *The New York Times*, May 10, 2023.

How to Win the Contest

1. Emma Allen, "The Cartoon Department Coup," *The New Yorker*, December 30, 2019.

2. "How Lazy Am I?," *The Cartoon Lounge*, season 4, episode 11.

3. "How to Win the Caption Contest," Cartoon Desk, *The New Yorker*, October 10, 2012. Mankoff subsequently expanded on that advice in his memoir, *How About Never? Is Never Good For You?—My Life in Cartoons*. He suggested verbalizing, conceptualizing, topicalizing, socializing, and fantasizing. If you want details, buy his book.

Who's Talking?

1. "For a while [Ross] had used a pencil as a pointer, but he was afraid of marking up the drawings. Then he tried a ruler, but the goddamn thing wasn't right, and fate directed him to the knitting needles that solved this little problem." James Thurber, *The Years with Ross* (Little, Brown & Co., 1957).

2. Thomas Vinciguerra, *Cast of Characters: Wolcott Gibbs, E.B. White, James Thurber and the Golden Age of The New Yorker* (W. W. Norton & Co., 2015).

3. *The New Yorker Cartoon Caption Contest Book: The Winners, the Losers, and Everybody In Between* (Andrews McMeel Publishing, 2008).

Make 'Em Laugh

1. Patrick House, "How to Win the New Yorker Cartoon Caption Contest," *Slate*, June 2, 2008. Since winning the contest, House has gone on to contribute several articles to *The New Yorker*, including "Werner Herzog Talks Virtual Reality," "What People Cured of Blindness See," and "The Brighter Side of Rabies."

2. *Comedians in Cars Getting Coffee*, season 6, episode 2.

3. https://www.imagination-institute.org.

4. "Your Caption Here," *The New Yorker*, April 24, 2005.

Make Sense

1. *Seinfeld*, season 9, episode 13 ("The Cartoon").

2. "Not Funny Enough? *New Yorker* Gives *Seinfeld* Cartoon a Second Chance," *Weekend Edition Sunday*, NPR, July 22, 2012.

3. "Not Funny Enough?" *Weekend Edition Sunday*, NPR, July 22, 2012.

Make the Speaker Oblivious

1. *30 Rock*, season 1, episode 2 ("The Aftermath").

Work on Your Delivery

1. "It Took This *New Yorker* Cartoonist 25 Years to Achieve His Childhood Dream," *Fresh Air*, NPR, March 7, 2022.

2. Cody Walker, "Captions in the Classroom," Cartoon Desk, *The New Yorker*, June 7, 2013.

Choose Your Words Carefully

1. *30 Rock*, season 3, episode 22 ("Kidney Now!").

2. *30 Rock*, season 6, episode 15 ("The Shower Principle").

3. "What's So Funny About Red?," *The New Yorker*, November 26, 2007.

4. "David Sipress: The Ink Spill Interview," *Ink Spill*, michaelmaslin.com, February 24, 2022.

Eliminate Unnecessary Words

1. "Your Caption Here," *The New Yorker*, April 24, 2005.

2. *The New Yorker Cartoon Caption Contest Book: The Winners, the Losers, and Everybody In Between* (Andrews McMeel Publishing, 2008), 80.

3. The prize for the longest *New Yorker* caption goes to Peter Arno, who, on November 18, 1933, abandoned his usual one-liners to deliver a four-paragraph joke that was funny only because it went on and on. The cartoon is set in a locker room, where a football coach is trying to shame his team to victory with a guilt-inducing half-time speech.

Punctuate Properly

1. "It Took This *New Yorker* Cartoonist 25 Years to Achieve His Childhood Dream," *Fresh Air*, NPR, March 7, 2022. The fact-checking department's obsession with cartoons can be traced back to Harold Ross, who once "doubted that the windows of the United Nations Building were anything like those shown in a drawing, and he ordered that a photographer be sent to take pictures of the windows." James Thurber, *The Years with Ross* (Little, Brown & Co., 1957).

2. Ana Marie Cox, "Bob Mankoff Thinks Cats Are Funnier Than Dogs," *The New York Times Magazine*, November 24, 2015.

No Exclamation Points!

1. Aimee Lee Ball, "Talking (Exclamation) Points," *The New York Times*, July 1, 2011.

2. Emma Goldberg, "Where Do We Stand on the Exclamation Point?," *The New York Times*, September 27, 2019.

3. Emma Goldberg, *The New York Times*, September 27, 2019.

4. Caitlin Dewey, "Donald Trump, Twitter, and the Art of the Exclamation Point," *The Washington Post*, July 22, 2016.

5. *Seinfeld*, season 5, episode 4 ("The Sniffing Accountant").

Don't Be Too Predictable

1. *The New Yorker Cartoon Caption Contest Book: The Winners, the Losers, and Everybody In Between* (Andrews McMeel Publishing, 2008), 72.

2. Mike Sacks, *Poking a Dead Frog: Conversations with Today's Top Comedy Writers* (Penguin Books, 2014).

3. "Your Caption Here," *The New Yorker*, April 24, 2005.

Don't Be Too Unpredictable

1. "Cracking the Code," Cartoon Desk, *The New Yorker*, June 1, 2011.

Don't Get Cute

1. P. J. O'Rourke, "The Pun's Story," *The New York Times*, April 15, 2011.

Think of Many Captions

1. "And the Winner Is," *The New Yorker*, February 7, 2000.

2. Keith Sawyer, "The New Yorker Cartoon Caption Contest," *The Creativity Guru*, keithsawyer.wordpress.com, October 23, 2009.

Don't Get Discouraged

1. Roger Ebert, "The New Yorker. No, The New Yorker," www.rogerebert.com, July 16, 2009.

2. Adam Martin, "Roger Ebert Wins New Yorker Cartoon Caption Contest," *The Atlantic*, April 25, 2011.

3. Roger Ebert, "Ebert's Moment of Glory: He *Finally* Wins Caption Contest," *Chicago Sun-Times*, April 27, 2011.

Don't Be Vulgar

1. Robert Mankoff, "Roger Ebert's Final Cartoon Captions," Cartoon Desk, *The New Yorker*, April 5, 2013.

2. Mary Norris, "Dropping the F-Bomb," *The New Yorker*, June 28, 2012.

3. John McPhee, "Editors & Publisher," *The New Yorker*, June 25, 2012.

4. Ian Frazier, "Easy Cocktails from the Cursing Mommy," *The New Yorker*, September 14, 2009.

5. Anthony Lane, "Space Case," *The New Yorker,* May 15, 2005.

6. Robert Mankoff, *The New Yorker Cartoon Caption Contest Book: The Winners, the Losers, and Everybody In Between* (Andrews McMeel Publishing, 2008).

7. RJ Casey, "Checking In with Zach Kanin," *The Comics Journal*, January 22, 2018.

Don't Be Shocking

1. Joshua Rothman, "Humor in *The New Yorker*," *The New Yorker*, November 20, 2012. *New Yorker* co-founder Harold Ross sometimes referred to his magazine as a "comic paper." Nancy Franklin, "Lady with a Pencil," *The New Yorker*, February 18, 1996.

2. Emma Allen, "Sam Gross Was Funny to the End," *The New Yorker*, May 8, 2023.

Get Out the Vote

1. Alex Altman, "How to Win the New Yorker Caption Contest," *Time*, June 8, 2009.

Summing Up

1. "Cracking the Caption Code," Cartoon Desk, *The New Yorker,* June 1, 2011.

Two Heads Are (Sometimes) Better Than One

1. Keith Sawyer, "The New Yorker Cartoon Caption Contest," *The Creativity Guru*, keithsawyer.wordpress.com, October 23, 2009.

Collaborating at *The New Yorker*

1. John Seabrook, "William Maxwell, the Art of Fiction," *The Paris Review*, no. 85 (Fall 1982).

2. *New Yorker* cartoonist Peter Kuper and I collaborated on a vulgar but loving tribute to that classic:

"I say it's broccoli, and I say 'fuck it.'"

The American Bystander, no. 5.

3. Thomas Kunkel, *Letters from the Editor: The New Yorker's Harold Ross* (Modern Library, 2001).

4. Michael Maslin, *Peter Arno—The Mad, Mad World of* The New Yorker's *Greatest Cartoonist* (Regan Arts, 2016).

5. Thomas Vinciguerra, *Cast of Characters: Wolcott Gibbs, E. B. White, James Thurber and the Golden Age of* The New Yorker (W. W. Norton & Co., 2015).

6. Michael Maslin, "Peter De Vries, Cartoon Doctor," *Ink Spill*, michaelmaslin.com, April 10 2013.

7. Jeffrey Frank, "Riches of Embarassment [*sic*]," *The New Yorker*, May 16, 2004.

8. Michael Maslin, michaelmaslin.com, April 10, 2013.

9. Michael Maslin, "Collaborating Cartoonists," *Ink Spill*, michaelmaslin.com, June 6, 2013.

10. My wife's friend Peter worked in a bookstore that had a strict policy against commenting on customers' purchases. He was tempted to violate this policy only once—when a man bought an issue of *Guns & Ammo* together with a book on anger management.

11. In 2019, Nell Scovell and I both contributed to *Esquire*'s annual "Dubious Achievements" feature, where one-sentence summaries of actual news stories from the past year appear under bold-faced headlines that satirize the event. *Esquire* provides the summaries, and contributing writers come up with the headlines. Scovell was asked to contribute because she's an accomplished humor writer. I was asked because Mankoff had just become the magazine's cartoon and humor editor, and he was again testing my abilities. I don't know which headlines Scovell submitted, but here were my contributions:

> **PRESIDENT HAILED FOR MINORITY APPOINTMENT** In a Fox News interview, seated next to his wife, Brett Kavanaugh volunteered (unprompted) that he was a virgin in high school "and many years thereafter."

> **TRUMP TO JOIN PUTIN, DUTERTE, AND ERDOGAN FOR "ORIGINAL STRONGMEN OF COMEDY" TOUR** During a September address to the United Nations General Assembly, President Trump's claim that his administration had accomplished more in two years than "almost any administration" in American history drew laughter.

> **I LIKE PEOPLE WHO WEREN'T CRUCIFIED** A former member of President Trump's Hispanic Advisory Council boasted that he could win reelection even against "a combined ticket of Jesus and the Virgin Mary."

> **ADMINISTRATION HOPES TO BOND JUST AS STRONGLY WITH IRAN** A U.S. State Department spokeswoman cited the D-Day invasion as an example of America's "very strong relationship" with Germany.

> **GERMANS PERFECTLY HAPPY TO BE KNOWN FOR HITLER AGAIN** A study found that upward of one hundred Germans die every year from risky masturbation practices.

> **PUBLIC-EDUCATION SYSTEM ADMIRES DOCK'S ABILITY TO WITHSTAND ASSAULT** A prankster unmoored Betsy DeVos's $40 million family yacht, setting it adrift on Lake Erie and causing $10,000 in damages.

"Dubious Achievements 2018," *Esquire*, Winter 2019.

12. Emma Allen, "So, You Want to Be a New Yorker Cartoonist," *The New Yorker*, June 6, 2021.

Gag Writer

1. *Everybody Loves Raymond*, season 1, episode 6 ("Frank the Writer").

Parallel Thinking

1. Robert Mankoff, *The New Yorker Cartoon Caption Contest Book: The Winners, the Losers, and Everybody In Between* (Andrews McMeel Publishing, 2008).

2. Emma Allen, "How Not to Write a Caption," *The New Yorker Radio Hour*, April 3, 2018.

Humor Is Subjective

1. "And the Winner Is," *The New Yorker*, February 7, 2000.

2. Robert Mankoff, "Anatomy of a New Yorker Cartoon," TED Salon, June 26, 2013.

3. "How Lazy Am I?," *The New Yorker's Cartoon Lounge*, season 4, episode 11.

4. *New Yorker Cartoon Caption Contest Podcast*, episode 85.

5. You can never be too careful, though. The stand-up comedian Marc Maron once did a bit about a sportscaster who kills himself after getting assigned to cover a miniature golf tournament, and an audience member whose brother had recently attempted suicide got on stage and tackled him. Incidents like that inspired the satirical newspaper *The Onion* to publish a fake op-ed by a man who, at a party, overheard some people talking and laughing about a scene from the movie *Police Academy*.

   > You know that part where the guy flies off the motorcycle handlebars, and he flies right at the horse's ass and gets his head stuck in it? Remember how funny you said that was? Well, I just want to say I didn't appreciate that too much, because my brother died that way.

   "That's Not Funny, My Brother Died That Way," *The Onion*, August 4, 1999.

6. Jay Dixit, "Wisecrackers—What Happens When You Hold a Mirror Up to Seven Comedians?," *Psychology Today*, September 1, 2008.

Anti-Humor

1. That cartoon did not appear in *The New Yorker*. It never would, but if you want to learn more about Callahan, whose controversial work sometimes led to protests and boycotts, watch the Gus Van Sant film, *Don't Worry, He Won't Get Far on Foot*, with Joaquin Phoenix as Callahan. The movie's title is a caption from one of Callahan's cartoons, which shows a posse of cowboys on horseback who come across an abandoned wheelchair in the desert. Callahan

was a quadriplegic, and his cartoons often took aim at his condition. His autobiography is entitled *Will the Real John Callahan Please Stand Up?*

2. The website's title is a reference to this drawing by Paul Noth, which was featured in Contest No. 247:

Andrew Steiner, of Bend, Oregon, submitted the winning caption: "*They'd probably be more fun if the barrel had air holes.*"

3. Andrea K. Scott, "Futurism," *The New Yorker*, May 23, 2011.

4. Robinson Meyer, "A New Caption That Works for Every New Yorker Cartoon," *The Atlantic*, September 22, 2015.

5. Denver Nicks, "This Genius Figured Out the Perfect Caption for Every New Yorker Cartoon," *Time*, September 23, 2015.

6. Ana Marie Cox, "Bob Mankoff Thinks Cats Are Funnier Than Dogs," *The New York Times*, November 24, 2015.

7. Robert Mankoff, "The Universal Caption," Cartoon Desk, *The New Yorker*, May 25, 2011.

8. Agarwal Aashna, "They Wanted to Win. Then They Made @ShittyNewYorkerCartoonCaptions," *Lithium*, February 4, 2021.

PUNS

1. "And The Winner Is. . . . ," *The New Yorker*, January 24, 2005.

2. Julie Beck, "Why Do Puns Make People Groan?," *The Atlantic*, July 10, 2015.

3. P. J. O'Rourke, "The Pun's Story," *The New York Times*, April 15, 2011.

4. "Best of the Caption Contest," *The New Yorker*, November 1, 2010.

RISE OF THE MACHINES

1. Kristen Scholer, "Tesla Stock Moves on April Fools' Joke," *The Wall Street Journal*, April 1, 2015.

2. David Marchese, "An A.I. Pioneer on What We Should Really Fear," *The New York Times Magazine*, December 21, 2022.

AFTERWORD

1. "Nobody Writes a Caption Like Larry Wood," *The New Yorker Radio Hour*, January 15, 2016.

2. *The New Yorker Cartoons of the Year 2015*.

3. In her initial sketch, Chast made me look much younger than I am for the reason she noted at the bottom of her drawing:

from left to right: Neima, me, Ed, Julia, Liana, Lawrence*, Emily
(* I have no idea what Lawrence looks like)

4. "Your Caption Here," *The New Yorker*, April 24, 2005.

5. In "The Impossible Caption Contest," Dahlia Gallin Ramirez created truly insurmountable challenges by drawing seventeen uncaptionable images, including an uninhabited desert island, a rock, and a therapy session where a doughnut and elephant float above a caveman who's telling his problems to a snake while, in the distance, Godzilla rampages through the city. *newyorker.com*, October 7, 2021.

About the Authors

Benjamin Schwartz

LAWRENCE WOOD has been a finalist in *The New Yorker* Cartoon Caption Contest a record-setting fifteen times and won eight contests. For more than twenty years he was a Lecturer in Law at the University of Chicago Law School, where he taught a class on housing and poverty law that Supreme Court Justice Antonin Scalia dismissed as a "waste of time." Lawrence is currently the supervising attorney at Legal Action Chicago.

BOB MANKOFF is a former cartoon editor for *The New Yorker*, where he worked for twenty years. He is the president of Cartoon Collections, the largest cartoon licensing source on the planet, and the author of numerous books, including his *New York Times* bestselling memoir *How About Never—Is Never Good for You?: My Life in Cartoons*.